Terrance Travel:

A Pocket Guide to

The Florida Keys

(Including the Everglades & Key West)

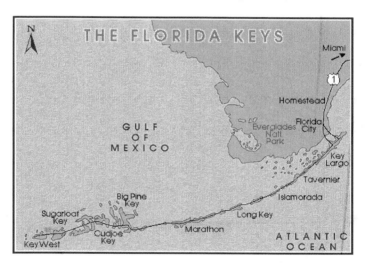

Terrance Zepke

Copyright © 2016 by Terrance Zepke

All queries should be directed to: www.safaripublishing.net

Library of Congress Cataloging-in-Publication Data

Zepke, Terrance

TERRANCE ZEPKE

Terrance Talks Travel: A Pocket Guide to the Florida Keys

America/Terrance Zepke p. cm.

ISBN: 978-1-942738-04-6

1. Travel-Florida. 2. Adventure Travel-Everglades. 3. Safari-Everglades. 4. Key West. 5. Florida Keys. 6. Florida Keys Wildlife. 7. Key Largo. 8. Florida Keys Guidebook. 9. Fishing-Florida Keys. 10. Scuba Diving-Florida Keys. 11. Florida Keys Attractions. 12. Beaches-Florida Keys. I. Title.

First edition

10 9 8 7 6 5 4 3 2 1

Safari Publishing

CONTENTS

Aerial View of Overseas Highway

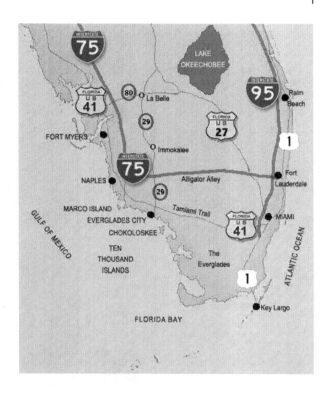

**The drive down the Overseas Highway
(U.S. 1) is pleasant and scenic. See what's
going on right now in the Florida Keys:**

http://www.fla-keys.com/webcams/

Introduction

There are many special places scattered across America, such as the Grand Canyon, Kauai, Monument Valley, and Cape Hatteras National Seashore. I probably can't name half of them. Suffice it to say we are blessed with many national treasures.

But there are only a handful of places that are so extraordinary that they are more than geographic locations and much more than their physical components. These extraordinary habitats feel as *alive* as if they had a pulse and heartbeat. The Florida Keys is such a place.

This skinny secession of islands is connected to the mainland and to one another by forty-two bridges and the Overseas Highway, which is an engineering marvel—even for the 21st century—and a breathtakingly scenic drive.

As you cross into the Keys, you enter another world—one you soon realize can never be tamed. We can erect buildings and bridges and attempt to civilize this place, but the Keys will never be like other communities—nor do we want it to be.

One reason is the people. Folks are different here—and proud of it. The Keys (and Key West in particular) is a mecca for free spirits and free thinkers. There is nothing conventional about this place or its people, who went so far as to briefly secede from America in 1982 to form the Conch Republic.

There are havens sprinkled all along the Keys, such as Big Cypress National Preserve, Key Deer Refuge, and John Pennekamp Coral Reef Park, which was the first undersea park in the U.S. and includes the only living coral barrier reef system in North America.

The world's only underwater hotel is here too. While you will need diving gear to get your room, you don't need waterproof luggage to stay in this one-of-a-kind sea lodge!

There are plants and habitats and wildlife that cannot be found anywhere else in the world except in the bizarre and beautiful Florida Keys.

Where else can you enjoy an exhilarating airboat ride through the gator-filled swamps, enjoy a conch train tour, and take part in a spectacular sunset celebration (that includes sword swallowers, unicyclists, and acrobats) all in the same afternoon?

The Florida Keys are located in the subtropics, making them more akin to the Caribbean than the rest of Florida or the U.S. Just how many keys exist is greatly disputed. The numbers range from 50 to 1,700, depending on the source.

But what can't be disputed is all they have to offer. Key Largo is the "Scuba Diving Capital of the World." Islamorada is the "Fishing

Capital of the World." Key West is the oldest and one of the best places to have a good time. One of my favorite shirts is a Key West t-shirt (pink, of course) I bought on Duval Street. Not only is it super comfy but it has a picture of a large umbrella drink on the front and is captioned *"It's 5 O'Clock Somewhere!"* You gotta love this place. It is full of fun, energy, and positivity.

Whatever you are looking for can be found here, such as all kinds of nightlife on Duval Street to dozens of art galleries where you can find everything from cheap ceramic light covers to expensive serigraphs and sculptures. There are so many yummy restaurants, cafes, food stands, and food trucks along the Keys that you will leave regretful that you didn't have time to sample more.

You may want to schedule your visit to coincide with one of their many fabulous festivals, such as Theater Festival, Fantasy Fest, Underwater Music Festival, International Sand Castle Competition and Hemingway Days.

Regardless of what you do while you're in the keys, you will leave knowing why so many came for a visit and never left—or you may choose to join the many who came for a vacation and ended up hunkering down in Paradise permanently.

Fast Facts

SIZE: The Florida Keys are made up of Upper, Middle, and Lower Keys. They are a coral cay archipelago on the southern coast of Florida. They begin roughly fifteen miles south of Miami and extend all the way to the Dry Tortugas. This skinny secession of islands divides the Atlantic Ocean from the Gulf of Mexico. The Florida Keys are comprised of many tiny islands with some being little more than sandbars, but an accurate count seems impossible. Sources vary from 50 – 1700.

DISTANCE: You will cross 42 bridges during your 110-mile journey over the Overseas Highway (U.S. 1) if you drive the whole distance. The highway has been designated a Scenic Byway. It is 59 miles from Miami to the first key, Key Largo. This drive can take 1-2 hours, depending on traffic. From Key Largo to Key West is 101 miles.

FYI: From Key West it is only 90 miles to Cuba.

POPULATION: While the rest of Florida is growing, the population of the Keys is shrinking. In 2000, the population was 79, 535 and the Census for 2010 was 73,090. The Keys strict building regulations, cost of living and a small number of high-paying jobs are the reasons for the decline. The majority of the population is white (84%) with 10% being African American and 6% being other races including Hispanic and Asian.

LANGUAGE: Conch! While the official language is English, residents of Key West call themselves "conchs" and they have fondly dubbed their utopia "The Conch Republic." You'll find a bit of everything here, from wild and crazy Hemingway and Jimmy Buffet types to the ultra-genteel. The Keys have international workers and visitors from all over the world and since it is in close proximity to the Caribbean you will also hear lots of different languages spoken, especially Spanish and French-Caribbean Creole.

CURRENCY: The U.S. dollar is the currency used throughout Florida. Credit cards are accepted most places. ATMs are widely available in Key West but less common on smaller keys. Cash and travelers checks are accepted everywhere. If you want to exchange foreign currency for U.S. currency the best place is at an Exchange Bureau at the Miami International Airport (MIA) or at a Miami bank. MIA has foreign currency exchange booths at four locations on the 2nd level throughout the terminal, two locations in each Greeter's Lobby areas (concourse E 1st level and concourse J 3rd level), and three locations passing security checkpoints: one inside concourse J, one location inside concourse D and

one location at E Satellite building.
http://www.miami-
airport.com/services_and_amenities.a
sp. There is an ATM in the Key West
EYW Airport. http://www.key-west-
international-airport. For more on
currency conversion, go to
www.oanda.com

TO GET THERE: Most
international flights arrive at Miami
International Airport (MIA).
www.miami-airport.com. However,
there are some flights that land at Key
West EYW Airport. www.key-west-
international-airport. There are rental
car counters at both airports. If you
are planning to rent a car you should
reserve it when you book your flight.
Additionally, there are some charter
flights into Florida Keys Marathon
Airport. http://www.monroecounty-
fl.gov/FAQ.aspx?QID=97.
There are several cruise ships
that dock at the port of Key West.
There is also a year-round ferry

service from Fort Myers to the Keys
aboard *Key West Express*. Passengers
arrive at the Key West Bight Ferry
Terminal in 3 - 3.5 hours.
www.seakeywest.com. Greyhound
Buses run from Miami and Fort
Lauderdale to Marathon and Key
West.

Experienced boaters can reach
the Florida Keys along the Atlantic
side of the Keys or by traveling on the
Gulf of Mexico side. The Intracoastal
Waterway from Miami passes through
Card and Barnes Sounds into Florida
Bay but this route is limited to 5-foot
draft vessels. The ocean side route is
Hawk Channel, a buoy marked
passage between the outermost reefs
and the Keys. Reservations must be
made in advance of your arrival at
area marinas.

Additionally, visitors can drive
to the Keys. As you can imagine, the
drive is scenic along the Overseas

Highway, which originates near Miami and ends at Key West. The drive begins at MM 126 at Florida City and ends at MM 0 in Key West. As you head down the Keys, Florida Bay/Gulf of Mexico is to your right and the Atlantic Ocean is to your left. If coming from Miami you should bypass the Miami traffic by taking I-95, I-75 or FL-836 to the Florida Turnpike (south). Card Sound Road offers an alternative route to Key Largo.

From Miami International Airport: Take LeJeune Road south to 836 West. Catch the Florida Turnpike south toward Key West, the Turnpike ends at US 1 in Florida City. Now follow U.S. 1 south about 22 miles to Key Largo.

From Ft. Lauderdale-Hollywood International Airport: Follow the signs for 595 West. Take 595 to the Florida Turnpike. The Turnpike ends at U.S. 1 in Florida City. Now follow U.S. 1 south into the Florida Keys.

From the north, take the Florida Turnpike south to just below Ft. Lauderdale, where Exit 4 (Homestead/Key West) joins the southern portion of the Turnpike, the Turnpike ends at US 1 in Florida City. Follow U.S. 1 south into the Florida Keys.

From Florida's West Coast: Take 1-75 Alligator Alley east to the Miami exit and then south to the Turnpike Extension. The Turnpike ends at U.S. 1 in Florida City. Follow U.S. 1 south into the Florida Keys.

Another option is to fly into Fort Lauderdale-Hollywood International Airport. It is 86 miles from the airport to Key Largo. This is the best option for those interested in visiting the Everglades or if you're interested in Fort Lauderdale area attractions.www.fortlauderdaleinternationalairport.com.

FYI: I highly recommend taking the Overseas Highway all the way down the Keys. It is the best way to see all the Keys have to offer. Did you know that the Overseas Highway is one of only thirty roads in America that have been accepted as National Scenic Byways?

Best Playlist for Florida Keys Roadtrip: Escape (The Pina Colada Song), Kokomo (or anything by the Beach Boys), Living on Key West Time, The Florida Keys Song, Don't Stop the Party, Hurricane Party (in the Florida Keys), Those Lazy-Hazy-Crazy Days of Summer, Some Beach, Nip Sip, No Shirt No Shoes No Problems, Sailing the Florida Keys, Summer Breeze, and anything by Jimmy Buffet, especially Key Largo, Margaritaville, and Let's Go Fishin'.

If you are in the Miami area you should plan to visit Coral Castle. It is one of the world's most mysterious accomplishments because it was built by one man using only homemade tools. Also, the story of why he came to build it is just as fascinating as how he did it. 28655 S. Dixie Highway, Miami, FL 33033. www.coralcastle.com.

State flag of Florida

Flag of the Florida Keys

BEST TIME TO GO: November – April is the dry season while May – October (especially August to October) is the rainy season and hurricane season. It is hot and humid during the summer months. The best bargains on lodging and vacation packages can be found between August and October since this is the low season. Availability and good pricing can be hard to achieve during special events, such as Hemingway Days (July), Fantasy Fest (October), and Pridefest (June).

High Season: January – April

Shoulder (low) Season: May – July & November - December

Off Season: August – October

AVERAGE TEMPERATURES:
The Keys have a subtropical climate with an annual daily average temperature of 78 degrees. They have wet summers and dry winters. Winters are a good time to visit given the pleasant temperatures and little rainfall.

It is gloriously sunny most of the time in the Florida Keys. Most of its thirty-eight inches of average rainfall occurs during the summer.

Check out www.weather.com to find up-to-date weather information for anywhere in the Florida Keys.

FYI: It is estimated that Key West is 1,699 miles from the Equator.

Average Keys Temperatures in Farenheit

January	70
February	71
March	73
April	77
May	80
June	82
July	84
August	84
September	83
October	79
November	74
December	71

*Information provided by Florida Keys Tourism. It is important to note that these are *averages*. Also, keep in mind that the Keys are a subtropical climate, meaning there is high humidity.

 *Warning:*

Hurricane season officially runs from June 1 – November 30. Hurricanes bring lots of rain, wind, and waves. Due to its location, many hurricanes have hit or impacted the Keys, including Category 5 Hurricane Wilma in 2005. The highest risk of hurricanes hitting the Keys is during September.

Seasons of Florida Keys...

SPRING: March, April, May

SUMMER: June, July, August

FALL: September, October, November

WINTER: December, January, February

BUDGET: This depends on what you're doing and where you're coming from. The cheapest option is to drive to the Keys. International airfares vary according to the departure city and time of year. Lodging costs vary according to selection. There are numerous options, ranging from camping to five-star resorts. Additionally, how much money you will need to budget depends on activities, entertainment, dining options, the length of stay, the number of adults and kids in your group, etc. You will get a better idea for this after you have read through this reference and determined your itinerary.

UNIQUE EXPERIENCES: There are lots of those, such as eco-tours, airboat rides, swamp safaris, and spending the night in the world's only underwater lodge, Jules Undersea Lodge, www.jul.com. More information on these options will be provided later in this reference.

FYI: Be prepared to stand in line to pose beside the famous Key West SOUTHERNMOST POINT buoy-shaped marker, which is located at the corner of South and Whitehead Streets.

Five Best Things about the Keys:

*Key West

*Wildlife, Parks & Refuges

*The Reef System

*Unusual activities& attractions, such as SNUBA, dolphin encounters, Theater of the Sea, slough slogging, and Jetpack Experiences.

*Stress is NOT permitted here. A laidback attitude prevails!

**Green Turtles are one of several turtle
species that inhabit the waters around the
Florida Keys.**

*   *   *

You will find maps of the Florida
Keys and Key West that you can
download to your mobile device at
http://floridakeyskeepsake.com/florid
a-keys-maps/

More Fun Facts...

Three types of habitats are found in the Florida Keys: **tropical hardwood hammocks, mangrove forests**, and **salt-water marshes**.

Duval Street in Key West is known as the longest street in the world because it runs from coast to coast.

Since the 1980's, approximately **23 artificial reefs** have been put in place in the Florida Keys. Most are sunken ships.

The second largest marine sanctuary in America is the **Florida Keys National Marine Sanctuary**, which includes all the keys except the Dry Tortugas. It extends 2,800 square miles. www.floridakeys.noaa.gov.

The state plant is the orange blossom.

The Keys rank as the **third largest reef system** and one of the most popular diving destinations in the world. The Florida Keys reef stretches 192 miles, from Virginia Key in Biscayne Bay to Dry Tortugas in the Gulf of Mexico. Christ of the Abyss Statue (Key Largo) is one of the top underwater attractions in the Keys. To find dive spots and shipwrecks, www.earth.google.com/ocean.

A little-known place to go is **Turtle Hospital** on Marathon. It is open to the public and offers three tours daily. www.turtlehospital.org.

This conch cottage is known as the **oldest house** in Key West and was built in 1829. It was home to wrecker Captain Francis B. Watlington, his wife Emeline, and their nine daughters. The property has three buildings, the main house, the kitchen house, and the exhibit pavilion. It is open to public and free. www.oirf.org.

Key West is the oldest key, **Key Largo** is known as the "Diving Capital of the World," and **Islamorada** is the "Sport Fishing Capital of the World."

Surprisingly, the largest resort in the
Keys is not in Key West. It is **Hawks
Cay Resort** on Duck Key.
https://www.hawkscay.com/

Key Biscayne is not one of the
Florida Keys, but the first of the
Atlantic barrier islands.

Florida Manatees are large, fully
aquatic, mostly herbivorous marine
mammals sometimes known as sea
cows. They measure up to thirteen
feet long, weigh as much as 1,200

pounds, and have paddle-like flippers. It has been difficult to get an accurate count of this species, but a 2016 count put the manatee population in Florida at about 6,000. They were recently moved from the endangered to the threatened list.

Florida Panther is the official state animal.

* * *

Florida Keys Historical Timeline

- 1513 – Florida was discovered by Spanish Explorer Ponce de Leon.
- 1815 – Spain gave this island (Key West) to Juan Pablo Salas for his service to his country.
- 1821 – Salas sold the island to John Simonton for $2,000.
- 1822 – U.S. Navy became interested in Key West as a naval base due to its unique location in the northern Caribbean.

- 1820s -1850s – Key West grew and became the richest city per capita in U.S. due to wrecking industry. Other budding industries included fishing, turtling, salt manufacturing, and cigar making.
- 1828 – Key West became incorporated.
- 1829 – First Post Office in the Florida Keys opens in Key West.
- 1832 – John J. Audubon is the first tourist to visit the Florida Keys.
- 1845 – Florida becomes 27th state.
- 1849 – Lucrative sponging industry sprang up in the Keys.
- 1855 – Population of the Keys was 2,700.
- 1867 – First public schools open in Key West.
- 1890 – Key West was the largest city in the state of Florida and known as the

sponging capital of the world. This was also the peak of cigar making with 129 factories here and 100,000 cigars produced a year.

- 1899 – The telephone comes to Key West.
- 1912 – Flagler Railroad was completed, which finally connected the Keys with the mainland.
- 1913 – First flight from Key West to Cuba happened.
- 1920's – Illegal rum running began because of Prohibition. Beer and rum were smuggled in from Cuba and whiskey and scotch from the Bahamas. This was a dangerous but highly profitable enterprise.
- 1928 – First car trip to Key West takes place. Hemingway makes his first visit to Key West.

- 1930s – The Keys were reinvented as a tourist destination in an effort to help the post-depression economy.
- 1930s – A submarine base was established with 25,000 military personnel stationed here.
- 1934 – The Keys population was 11,000.
- 1935 – Hurricane hits Islamorada and kills 400-600 people and destroys the railroad.
- 1938 – Overseas Highway opens, once again connecting the Keys to the mainland.
- 1942 – First water pipeline reaches Key West from the mainland.
- 1950's – Electricity and road system reach Florida Keys.
- 1955 – Key Deer Refuge was established on Big Pine Key.
- 1960 – John Pennekamp State Park opens (first underwater

park in U.S.) and the Beatles visit Sugarloaf Key.

- 1970's – Indian Key purchased by the State of Florida and designated a state historic site.
- 1971 – First treasure from the *Atocha* found by Mel Fisher near Key West.
- 1974 – Navy base closed, resulting in economic disaster for the Keys.
- 1979 – First Fantasy Fest is held.
- 1980s – The island became known as a popular tourism destination.
- 1985 – All harvesting of conch in the Florida Keys is prohibited by law.
- 1990 – The Florida Keys were declared a National Marine Sanctuary.

- 1998 – Islamorada incorporates and becomes the Village of Islands.
- 2000 – U.S. census shows 79,589 residents in the Florida Keys.
- 2010 – U.S. census shows drop in population to 73,090.

The Mockingbird is Florida's state bird.

* * *

Best Beaches in the Keys

Anne's Beach (Islamorada). This is a really nice beach with a lovely boardwalk, restrooms, and lounge. There are no concessions but on the plus side, pets are welcome. MM 73.5.

Bahia Honda State Park (Big Pine Key). Known as one of the best beaches in America, it is a great place to go snorkeling and swimming. It's hard to explain why the beach is so great except to say that the colors— from the ocean to the sky—seem more vivid—and blue, blue, blue! It also has nature trails and a hidden beach that is smaller than the main one but just as lovely and more private. An admission fee is charged to enter the 524-acre park but it is well worth it. There are boat ramps, kayak rentals, great fishing, hiking, snorkeling trips, and more. MM 37.

Clarence S. Higgs Memorial Beach on Atlantic Boulevard (Key West). This is the second largest beach in Key West. Tucked away between White Street Pier and Casa Marina, this beach has a playground, bicycle paths, volleyball area, tennis, snorkeling, picnic area, and restaurant. West Martello Fort is located here.

Coco Plum Beach (Marathon) is very popular with the locals. It has chickees, which resemble little grass huts. These enclosures are available to everyone on a first come basis. There is ample parking and restrooms. This is a turtle nesting area (April – October) so please be respectful. MM 55.

Dog Beach is at Vernon and Waddell Streets in Key West. It is one of the few beaches in the Keys (and the only one in Key West) that permits dogs.

Fort Zachary Taylor Historic State Park is on the outermost tip of Key West. Many weddings have been held here at this scenic site. In addition to the beach, visitors can explore the old fort. There is a café and picnic area.

Holiday Isle Beach Resort (Islamorada). This full-service resort has a beach that is open to the public, pools, shops, restaurants and bars, marina, watersports rentals (boats, jet skis, etc.), and fishing and diving charters. MM 84 in the Holiday Isle Complex.

Library Beach (Islamorada) is combination park and beach and has a picnic area with grill, playground, and

chickee (looks sort of like a tiki hut).
MM 81.5.

Little Duck Key Beach (Big Pine
Key). This is a small but beautiful
beach. Visitors can swim, sunbathe,
and enjoy its picnic area. MM 39.

Simonton Street Beach is in the
heart of Key West's Old Town.
Visitors will enjoy the view of Key
West Harbor and its convenient
location. Food, drink, and gear can be
found at Lagerheads Beach Bar &
Watersports.

Smathers Beach is on the south side
on South Roosevelt Boulevard in Key
West. It is one of the biggest beaches
on the island. Watersports equipment
and beach chair rentals are available,
as well as concession stands and food
trucks.

Sombrero Beach (Marathon). This
is a big beach that includes restrooms
and showers, playground, volleyball

courts, and picnic pavilions. Handicap accessible. This is a turtle nesting beach so please be respectful during nesting season (April – October). MM 50.

South Beach is at the end of the best-known street in Key West—Duval Street. It is a good spot to swim, sunbathe, and relax before hitting Duval Street attractions.

The Everglades

On route to The Keys, you'll pass through Homestead and Florida City on an eighteen-mile stretch of US 1 through the Everglades. Locals call this **"The Stretch."**

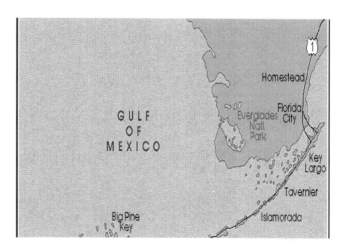

You'll want to spend some time here as this is one of the best places in America for eco-tours and adventures.

Most of the Upper Keys are located on the southeast border of the Everglades National Park. The Keys and the Everglades are in Monroe County.

Check out these webcams of the Everglades:

https://www.nps.gov/ever/learn/photosmultimedia/webcams.htm

With 1.5 million acres of swamps sub-tropical jungles and saw-grass prairies, Everglades National Park is one of the top "must see" parks in the U.S. *Did you get that?* It extends 1.5 million acres! It is a UNESCO World Heritage Site, Wetland of International Importance, and International Biosphere Reserve. Only three places in the world are on all three of these significant lists.

Everglades National Park was established in 1934. It is the third largest park in the United States. It is also home to 36 protected species, such as the West Indian Manatee, American Crocodile, and the Florida Panther. More than 350 species of birds can be found here, as well as 300 species of fish, 50 species of reptiles, and 40 mammal species.

Habitats found within the Everglades include Cypress Swamps,

Pinelands, Open-water Sloughs,
Hardwood Hammocks, Sawgrass
Marshes, and Mangrove Swamps.

Be sure and grab a bite to eat
before entering the Everglades
National Park as food options are
limited. An icon of Everglades City is
the **Seafood Depot**. Located inside a
1928 train depot, the restaurant is not
only a classic example of early
Florida architecture, but it also offers
spectacular views of the Everglades
and has a nice menu.102 E.
Broadway. Another good option is
Capri Restaurant. This cozy family-
owned restaurant has a varied menu,
serving fresh local seafood, steaks,
pork, veal, pizza, pasta, and classic
Italian dishes. 935 N. Krome Ave.,
Florida City, FL 33034.
www.dinecapri.com. **Camelia Street**

Grill offers American and Mediterranean cuisine. 202 Camelia Street. http://www.yelp.com/biz/camellia-street-grill-everglades-city. Lastly, **City Seafood Restaurant & Market** is an option. Be forewarned that the menu is 99% seafood, specializing in stone crabs. They also sell fresh seafood, including stone crabs. You can take it with you or have it shipped home. Begonia Street. http://www.cityseafood1.com/.

Time permitting, you may want to visit the **Everglades Museum** while in Everglades City. Located in the center of town, it gives visits a good glimpse into the history of this region. FREE. 105 W. Broadway.

FYI: A recent survey taken by Recreational Boating and Fishing Foundation found the anglers and boaters rank the Florida Everglades the #1 fishing destination in America. Bahia Honda State Park on Pine Key (Lower Keys) was chosen as #2.

There are four visitor centers in the
Everglades National Park: Ernest F.
Coe Visitor Center, Flamingo, Shark
Valley, and Gulf Coast (Chekika).
Entrance fees are collected at Shark
Valley and Ernest F. Coe Visitor
Center (Homestead), which is the
main entrance to the park. Be advised
that at the time of publication Chekika
was closed indefinitely due to budget
cuts. It is a good idea to check their
hours of operation before your visit.

Be prepared to take some kind
of tour if you want to get the most out
of the experience. Plan to take a tram
ride through Shark Valley, or a boat

ride on Florida Bay, or even a walk on one of the boardwalk trails will get you closer to nature. You can also hike, bike, canoe, and kayak along the scenic waterways. https://www.nps.gov/ever/planyourvisit/visitorcenters.htm.

Hopefully, you will see lots of wading birds and other wildlife, such as deer and gators.

If you're interested in camping, primitive camping is available but better options are Long Pine Key and

Flamingo. They have some amenities, such as electric hookups (tent and trailer sites), showers, restrooms, picnic tables, grills, and drinking water. While Flamingo has more amenities, Long Pine Key got better reviews on TripAdvisor.
http://www.nps.gov/ever/planyourvisit/camping.htm

The best place to bike is at Shark Valley or at Long Pine Key Nature Trail. The Everglades offers a 15-mile paved road that is flat and free of rough terrain. Allow a couple of hours so that you can stop and enjoy the scenery and wildlife along the way. If you want to rent a bike (children's bikes and child seats are available) you can do that at Shark Valley Tram Tours.
http://www.sharkvalleytramtours.com

FYI: www.BikeTours.com and www.Backroads.com both offer a six-day guided Keys tour but you better be in good shape. Participants bike an average of 28 miles every day and when you're not biking you're walking!

If you're interested in canoeing or kayaking, be advised that the Wilderness Waterway is 99 miles long. It takes up to ten days to complete it. However, shorter trails are available and well-marked. Information, rentals and guided tours are available at http://evergladesadventures.com/ http://evergladeskayakcompany.com/ and https://www.zerve.com/d/everglades-naples/canoe-rentals.

Unusual activities can be accomplished too, such as geocaching and slough slogging. Geocaching (https://www.nps.gov/ever/planyourvi sit/geocaching.htm) is a real-world outdoor treasure hunt. Players must find hidden geocaches using state-of-the-art technology. There is nothing techie about slogging. This is when participants go off official trails into the slough to get up close to wildlife. https://www.nps.gov/ever/planyourvis it/sloughslog.htm.

But I think the best way to explore the Everglades (if you have to pick just one) is a boat tour. There are lots of options so I recommend you check TripAdvisor for traveler recommendations and also http://www.nps.gov/ever/planyourvisi t/things2do.htm.

I recommend **Everglades Eco-Tours** as I have used them and had a great experience. They offer a great full-day Everglades & Florida Bay Ecology Tour. Roundtrip transportation from Fort Myers and Fort Lauderdale area is available. A highly-trained naturalist guide leads every tour. Included with this eco-tour is a nature walk, delicious lunch (including fried alligator bites), scenic boat cruise into the Ten Thousand Islands mangrove forest inside the park, and a wildlife drive through Big Cypress National Preserve. The highlight is an airboat ride through sawgrass prairies and pond apple forests. You also see a lot of other fun stuff as you crisscross this region and the guide shares lots of cool trivia and happily answers all questions. www.ecosafari.com.

Here's my advice: Wear 30 SPF sunscreen, bug spray, hat, and comfortable walking shoes (no flip flops). Don't bother primping as the wind (airboat) and humidity (everywhere) makes that a waste of time. You will be given earplugs as you board the airboat but don't panic. They aren't necessary if you avoid the very back of the boat. Approximately one million visitors come to the Everglades each year. This means you need to make reservations BEFOREHAND if you want to be guaranteed a space. You can go on your own but it will still be crowded and you may not be able to get a boat ride, at least not without a lengthy wait. Tour groups don't wait. As soon as we were all assembled on the dock, we took off.

Tipping is expected EVERYWHERE in Florida. Tour guides, boat captains, trolley drivers, ghost walk leaders, bus drivers, and everyone else who interacts with tourists expects a tip. In case you

forget, don't worry. There are signs
posted everywhere to remind you that
"Tips are welcome."

The company has an alternative
to this adult-oriented tour if you're
traveling with small kids. Captain
Bob's Excellent Adventure is shorter
(half-day) and kid-oriented with an
interactive reptile show. More options
can be found at
http://www.viator.com/Everglades-
National-Park-tours/Eco-
Tours/d5286-g9-c119.

FYI: The Everglades has two seasons: a dry
season and a wet season. The dry season
lasts from November to March and the wet
season lasts from April to November. The
dry season is also the busy season because
of the warm winters that attract the largest
variety of wading birds and their predators,
such as mangrove cuckoo, American White
Pelican, Black-crowned Night Heron, Bald

Eagle, Peregrine Falcon, Great Horned Owl, Osprey, and Black Vulture. The wet season is wet, buggy, humid, hot, and many ranger programs are not offered. It is not a good time to visit. For more about Everglades National Park, http://www.nps.gov/ever/index.htm

Alligator Farm is open daily and has snake and alligator shows, alligator feedings, airboat rides, and more than 2,000 alligators. 40351 SW 192 Avenue, Homestead, FL 33034. http://www.everglades.com/

Big Cypress National Preserve is just north of Everglades National Park on Florida's southwest coast. In addition to lots of flora and fauna and giant Cypress trees, it is home to all kinds of wildlife, such as the Florida panther, deer, wild hogs, and many species of birds. Visitors can hike the Florida National Scenic Trail on their own or on a ranger-guided nature walk. Big Cypress National Preserve encompasses 729,000 acres of swamp land. MM 54, U.S. 41. Open every day year-round. www.nps.gov/bicy. **Big Cypress Welcome Center** is at 33000 Tamiami Trail East, Ochopee, Florida 34141. https://www.nps.gov/bicy/planyourvis it/big-cypress-swamp-welcome-center.htm

Big Cypress Seminole Indian Reservation has a large museum. The Ah-Tah-Thi-Ki Museum has more than 30,000 artifacts. In addition to its many exhibits, visitors may visit the Seminole Village, Clan Pavilion,

Ceremonial Grounds, and Cypress Dome with boardwalk. There is also a store that sells arts and crafts and more. Swamp safaris, airboat rides, animal exhibits, and critter shows are offered. Open every day. http://www.ahtahthiki.com.

Biscayne National Park is south of Miami and east of Homestead. The visitor center is located on the mainland while much of the park is accessible only by boat. Numerous activities are available and the park is a definite must see for anyone interested in the offshore wonders of South Florida. 9700 SW 328 Street Homestead, Florida 33033. https://www.nps.gov/bisc/index.htm

Ochopee Post Office is the smallest post office in America. It is absolutely adorable! It is located between Big

Cypress National Preserve and the
Gulf Coast section of the Everglades
National Park.
http://www.floridarambler.com/histori
c-florida-getaways/ochopee-smallest-
post-office-everglades/.

Robert Is Here Fruit Stand & Farm
is at 19200 SW 344 Street,
Homestead, FL 33034. Visitors will
enjoy delicious fresh fruit milkshakes
and they can also buy fresh jams, fruit
and more. www.robertishere.com.

Tropical Everglades Visitor Center
provides information on area
attractions, lodging, restaurants, and
trail destinations. Open daily. 160 SE
1st Ave., Florida City, FL 33034. It is
located where the Florida Turnpike

ends and becomes US 1.
www.tropicaleverglades.com

Highlights:

The Seafood Depot, Robert Is Here Fruit Stand,
Alligator Farm, Big Cypress National Preserve, Big
Cypress Welcome Center, Everglades National Park,
Tropical Everglades Visitor Center, Ochopee Post
Office, Big Cypress Seminole Indian Reservation,
Shark Valley (ENP), Homestead, Everglades City,
Capri Restaurant, Wilderness Waterway, Biscayne
National Park, Florida City, and Everglades
Museum.

http://florida-everglades.com/

FLORIDA
KEYS

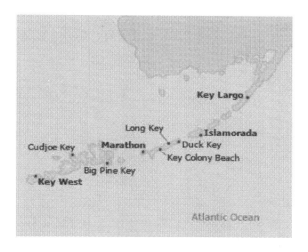

The Keys reef extends 192 miles from Biscayne Bay to the Dry Tortugas. It ranks as the third largest reef system and one of the most popular diving spots in the world. If you want to find the best Keys diving spots check out this map at http://www.google.com/earth/explore/showcase/ocean.html#tab=dive-spots.

The Keys were discovered in the 1500s but remained unsettled for hundreds of years. During this time they were home to pirates, Calusa Indians, and Spanish settlers. Now they host tourists from all over the world.

The Keys have just about everything vacationers could want, from sportfishing to eco-adventures. If you like to party, Key West is the place to go. If you're looking for a good family destination, Marathon is perfect. If you're searching for a little peace and quiet, Big Pine is a good choice. And the best place for snorkeling and diving is Key Largo.

The thing that's great about the Keys is that there is something for everyone and every budget. Visitors can opt to stay in campgrounds, lodges, inns, B & B's, mom and pop motels, resort hotels, guest cottages, condos, villas, and vacation rentals. Be aware that you'll pay top dollar December – April and some other times according to special events.

Be sure you do diligent research before booking any vacation property. Pay with a credit card and verify their license (All legitimate Florida vacation rentals must be licensed). Use common sense. If you have any doubts or suspicions about the property, don't book it. If you need help, The Florida Keys has an online chat link at the top of the home page at www.fla-keys.com and also the Lodging Association of the Florida Keys and Key West http://www.keyslodging.org/. I saw some good options on www.airbnb.com including an adorable cottage in Deer Key Refuge for a reasonable rate.

There are activities for all ages and interests, including shark cage diving (http://keyssharkdiving.com/), snorkeling, diving without an oxygen tank (this is an extreme sport that should not be undertaken by amateurs), banana boat rides, knee boarding, fishing, wakeboarding, kayaking, biking, hiking, boat eco-tours, jeep safaris, airboat rides, wingsuit flying, parasailing

(www.keywestsebago.com), jet
skiing, golf, tennis, skydiving,
kiteboarding, waterskiing, horseback
riding, nature walks, and more. For a
complete list of guides and outfitters
visit www.floridakeys.com.

So come with me as I take you
on a journey of discovery of one of
the most exceptional places in
America…

*FYI: These reefs provide $2.8 billion a year
to the Florida economy, mostly from tourists
who come to dive and fish.*

FYI: You will notice that there is a <u>green</u> marker sign for every mile along the Overseas Highway. This creates an easy-to-navigate system. Visitors will see little green signs that begin at Florida City (MM 127) and extend all the way to Key West (MM 0, pictured here). Mile markers let visitors know where they are and how to find a certain place. The Overseas Highway has been compared to being on a town's Main Street. You get on it and follow the mile marker signs and you can't get lost.

UPPER KEYS

Key Largo

The first key you come to is Key Largo, which is also the largest. This 33-mile long was originally called "Cayo Largo" (long island) by the Spanish explorers who discovered it.

The beginnings of a community was in 1870 when a post office was established. The population at that time was 60. Within twenty years the population had more than doubled. Train service from Miami to the Middle Keys (Marathon) began in 1908. There were four stations at Key Largo with a telegraph station inside one of the train stations. By 1912, the railroad extended all the way to Key West.

It was 1921 before the name officially changed to Key Largo. There were several commercial businesses in Key Largo by the early 1900s, including a hotel, newspaper, ice company, fishing lodge, packing house, and a handful of stores. The first subdivision, Key Largo City Gardens, was built in 1923. By 1930, there were 123 subdivisions in various planning stages but many never got built due to a 1929 hurricane and the collapse of the Great Florida Land Boom.

Key Largo's economy now relied on its citrus crops, which was mostly grapefruit and key limes. This was later replaced by tourism. The Upper Keys became known as a great fishing destination. A 1935 hurricane destroyed the railroad and hurt tourism until the overseas highway was completed.

The famous film, *Key Largo*, boosted tourism. Its biggest growth spurt occurred during the 1950s, thanks to electricity, water pipeline, mosquito control, the end of World War II, and the opening of a public high school.

Nowadays, Key Largo needs no

movie to call attention to itself. It is well-known, thanks in large part to it being dubbed "The Diving Capital of the World." (www.fla-keys.com/diving). In addition to lots of natural reefs, there are plenty of artificial reefs too, including the wreck of the *Spiegel Grove*, a 510-foot Navy ship intentionally sunk in 2002. All of these reefs create the perfect atmosphere to draw diverse and spectacular marine life.

In addition to plenty of water activities and nature tours, there is the **Key Largo Art Gallery** at MM 103.2 and there are lots of specialty shops, bars, and restaurants here, such as **Shell World** has a huge collection of shells and specialty gifts (www.shellworldflkeys.com), **Key Largo Chocolates** has everything chocolate you can dream of, including fudge key lime pie on a stick and free samples (www.keylargochocolates.com), The Island Smoke Shop has the largest

walk-in humidor in South Florida
(www.islandsmokeshop.com), and for
dining and chilling there are lots of
places like **Caribbean Club**
(www.caribbeanclubkl.com), **The
Fish House** (www.fishhouse.com),
Backyard Café (signature sandwich
is a lobster BLT,
www.keylargofisheries.com), and
**Jimmy Johnson's Big Chill at
Fisherman's Cove**
(www.jjsbigchill.com). Some
recommendations: Bimini conch
chowder, parmesan crusted snapper
(fresh yellowtail snapper encrusted in
parmesan cheese and buttermilk batter
and then topped with lump crab in a
lemon butter burre blanc), mango
coleslaw and a four-layer chocolate
overload cake! For possible celebrity
sightings, as well as fresh fish,
yellowtail snapper, stone crab claws,
and Florida lobster tails, visit
Snapper's Oceanfront Restaurant

& Tiki Bar.
www.snapperskeylargo.com.

FYI: Pictured here is the Largo Sound Rock Castle (Not to be confused with a replica that was built in Homestead). Built in 1920, its walls are three feet thick at ground level and taper to 16 inches at the top. This Key Largo coral castle has been dubbed the "Haunted House on Largo Sound" because it is reportedly haunted. It is one of the oldest structures still standing on the Upper Keys. Most have been destroyed by hurricanes or neglect. It is not open to the public—except for ghosts! MM 103.5 (Ocean Drive)

Conch Chowder

I thought it might be nice to include a local recipe or two in this book. Since I like Conch Chowder, I decided that would be a good one to include. I was shocked to discover that Conch Chowder is a lot of trouble to make. For one thing, it requires a lot of ingredients and the combined prep and cooking time is about six hours. That rules me out but for those who are willing to spend the time and take the effort, here's a good recipe I found on Food.com.

Ingredients (10 servings):

- 1 teaspoon olive oil
- 2 ½ cups chopped sweet onions
- 1 large bell pepper, chopped (about 1 cup)
- 1 cup lean ham, diced
- 2 large garlic cloves, minced

- 2 (14 1/2 ounce) cans chopped tomatoes
- 1 can (6 ounces) tomato paste
- $\frac{1}{2}$ cup tomato juice
- 1 cup hot water (I use broth)
- 1 bay leaf
- 1 tablespoon barbecue sauce
- 1 teaspoon marjoram
- $\frac{1}{2}$ teaspoon sage
- $\frac{1}{4}$ teaspoon thyme
- 1 teaspoon parsley
- $\frac{1}{2}$ teaspoon oregano
- $\frac{3}{4}$ teaspoon salt
- $\frac{1}{2}$ teaspoon cracked black pepper
- $\frac{1}{4}$ teaspoon cayenne pepper
- 1 -2 lb. tenderized ground conch

Place olive oil, onions, bell peppers, ham and garlic in a large soup pot over medium-high heat. Sauté, stirring occasionally, for 5 minutes or until onion is translucent. Add tomatoes, tomato paste, tomato juice, hot water, bay leaf, barbecue sauce, marjoram, sage, thyme, parsley, oregano, salt, cracked and cayenne peppers. Stir to combine ingredients and bring mixture to a boil.

Add conch to the pot. Reduce heat to low and simmer, covered, for 5 to 6 hours or until conch is tender.

Optional: Lace each serving with hot pepper sherry to taste.

Florida Keys Seafood Glossary:

Conch: Most likely the conch you'll be served will be imported from the Bahamas because Florida conch is endangered. I am told they taste the same, but since I have only had Caribbean conch I'll have to take their word for it. *Warning!* Conch is an acquired taste. Most folks don't love it immediately as it is a bit tough and has a different taste but you should definitely try it for yourself. Cracked conch (meaning pounded conch meat) that is breaded and fried is served as conch fritters and conch chowder is offered at many eateries throughout the Keys. A great deal depends on how the conch is prepared and by whom. I don't care for conch fritters but I like conch chowder if the cook makes it right.

Florida Lobster (spiny lobster): These are somewhat different from Maine lobsters. For one thing, they are clawless and have a slightly different texture. But if cooked right, they are tasty. Lobster season is August – March.

Grunts: These fish (see photo) are popular in the Keys but you won't find them listed on tourist menus except as "grunts and grits."

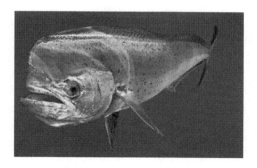

Mahi Mahi: Many folks confuse this with Flipper but Mahi Mahi is a type of fish, *Coryphaena hippurus*. It is distantly related to perch fish and not related in any way to the kind you see at Sea World, which are air-breathing mammals! It is commonly served blackened, Cajun-style, and grilled.

Shark: You will typically find shark on a "specials" menu and usually it is grilled.

Shrimp: You'll find lots of shrimp dishes served in most Keys restaurants as shrimp is plentiful and popular here. The most well-known are the Tortuga Pink Shrimp (also known as Key West Pink Shrimp), which is harvested from shrimp beds around the Dry Tortugas. Yum!

FYI: Be prepared to go on a diet when you get back from your vacation as you can't help but indulge in all the great food offered throughout the Keys!

Special Events: One of the biggest is the **Humphrey Bogart Film Festival** (October), which includes movie screenings, a gala, and more. www.bogartfilmfestival.com. However, my favorite is the **Anything That Floats Regatta Race** (August). Yes, it is what it sounds like. The rules are simple. Crews of two or more people are expected to reuse, recycle and regenerate floatable items found around the house to construct their boats. Oars and paddles are allowed to help navigate a half-mile buoyed course along Blackwater Sound from Key Largo's Caribbean Club to Sundowners and back. This is a sight to see! http://keylargoanythingthatfloatsrace.com/.

Other noteworthy events include **Key Largo Fourth of July Family Picnic and Parade and Fireworks, Key**

Largo's Original Music Festival (May), and **Capt. Slate's Underwater Easter Egg Hunt** (April). www.keylargochamber.org/events

African Queen is the boat that was used in the filming of the famous movie, *African Queen* (1951), starring Humphrey Bogart and Katherine Hepburn. To be honest, I was disappointed when I saw it. I hadn't seen the movie and had a different idea in my head. But in reality, the *African Queen* is small (only twelve feet long) and lacking in "bells and whistles." The boat can be rented for private parties and outings. Holiday Inn Marina. www.africanqueenflkeys.com. MM 100.

Dagny Johnson Key Largo Hammock Botanical State Park is

1,000 acres of tropical hardwood forest that was spared from development after a lengthy legal battle. Visitors may take a self-guided two-mile nature walk. Plan to bring bug spray and anything else you may need as there are no concessions here. This park is located on County Road 905. MM 106. www.floridstateparks.org/keylargohammock/

Florida Keys National Marine Sanctuary is one of 14 marine protected areas that make up the National Marine Sanctuary System, which includes John Pennekamp Coral Reef State Park. Located six miles offshore, it offers some of the best diving in the area. Highlights include *Spiegel Grove* (a 510-foot former US Navy ship), *Benwood Wreck* (WWII shipwreck), *Bibb* and *Duane* (Coast Guard cutters sunk), **Statue of Christ** of the Abyss (bronze

statue at Key Largo Dry Rocks reef can be easily viewed by snorkelers too), **Molasses Reef** and **The Elbow Reef** have several shipwrecks that draw lots of marine life including moray eels and barracuda.
http://floridakeys.noaa.gov/

FYI: To participate in charter dives, you will need a PADI certification. If you are not certified you can take a short training course in the Keys if you have 2-3 days. Or you can participate in a resort dive which does not require certification. You will take a brief training course and be accompanied by certified divers. You cannot scuba dive alone but you shouldn't anyway if you're not fully trained and certified. You don't need any training to snorkel but you will need to bring equipment or rent locally.

Another option is SNUBA (Surface Nexus Underwater Breathing Apparatus). This is when you dive without a tank on your back. Instead, it floats on the surface and is attached to you via a long tube. No certification is required but you are limited in how far you can dive and where you can dive. Currently, SNUBA is only permitted in the Lower Keys.

Whether snorkeling, diving or doing SNUBA, please do not touch the coral reefs. Human touch has been proven to cause damage to coral plants unless they're artificial.

Reef Etiquette

*Don't stand or rest on coral — if you need to adjust your gear, float on your back or in a seated position. If you need to stand, return to your boat.

*Maintain buoyancy — streamline gear, and use proper dive posture, with feet elevated slightly above the head.

*Secure all equipment — make sure it does not come in contact with the reef. Avoid wearing gloves in coral reef environments.

*Keep your distance — maintain a comfortable distance, and avoid very shallow areas, especially at entry and exit points.

*Leave marine life alone — do not touch, handle, feed or ride marine life. You are in their home.

*Keep the reef at the reef — animals or corals from the reef are not souvenirs. Remember, it is illegal to harvest coral in Florida.

*Look but don't touch — even a minor brush with a hand, fins or other dive and snorkel equipment can damage sensitive corals.

Harry Harris State Park is a picturesque park with a beach, playground, lagoon, restrooms, boat ramp, and picnic area. It is open daily free of charge but there is a small fee for everyone over the age of 12 to enter on weekends and holidays. MM 92.5.

John Pennekamp Coral Reef State Park is our country's only underwater park. It consists of nearly 54,000 acres of submerged land and 2,300 acres of uplands. It is one of the most visited attractions in the Keys so go early as the gates close when the park reaches maximum capacity, which can be as early as 10 a.m. Highlights include Coral Reef Theater, scuba diving and snorkeling (This reef is home to more than 600 species of tropical fish), glass bottom boat tours (aboard the large catamaran, *Spirit of Pennekamp*), kayaking and canoeing, fishing, Pennekamp Beach, and special programs, such as nature walks and campfire talks. The visitor center features several exhibits, an aquarium, and theater. There is a fee to enter the park and it varies according to whether you're a bicyclist, pedestrian, motorcyclist, or vehicle. There are also additional fees for activities, such as boat tours and kayak rentals. MM 102.5.

www.pennekamppark.com.
     Note: Camping is permitted in the park but reservations must be made through www.reserveamerica.com. More camping options can be found at the end of this chapter.

FYI: John Pennekamp Coral Reef State Park and Key Largo National Marine Sanctuary comprise 190 square miles of coral reefs, seagrass beds, and mangrove swamps. This includes 55 types of coral and 600+ species of fish, as well as many types of shorebirds and other native wildlife. Best ways to explore this park include a tour aboard the glass-bottomed boat, Spirit of Pennekamp, scuba diving at Molasses Reef, and snorkeling. The best option is to sign up for a half day or full day snorkeling outing with a local company, such as www.captainslate.com. Most accept all ages and have equipment you can rent.

Jules Undersea Lodge is the only underwater lodge in the world. I love this place and the best part is that you don't have to be certified to stay here as long as you complete a short diving course in the lagoon. You are then permitted to dive the 21' to your room. Jules Lodge is located in a tropical mangrove of the Emerald Lagoon. Certified divers are permitted to come and go as they please and will appreciate its proximity to John Pennekamp Coral Reef State Park. The lodge offers different packages to choose from, including a three-hour package rather than an overnight stay. There are two bedrooms, TV, DVD, stereo, galley, air conditioning, and a gourmet dinner is included. www.jul.com. MM 103.2 (51 Shoreline Drive).

Swimming with dolphins. There are three places that offer different dolphin encounters: Dolphin Cove, www.dolphincove.com; Dolphins Plus Research Center, www.dolphinsplus.com; and Dolphin Research Center, www.dolphins.org.

Wild Bird Rehabilitation Center is also a bird sanctuary and nature center. They offer guided tours around the Florida Bay. It is free but donations are accepted. www.fkwbc.org. MM 93.6.

FYI: When Key Largo's Jewfish Creek Bridge is raised during peak season, traffic on both sides of US 1 can back up for several miles.

Three Fun Facts About Key Largo

*Key Largo is home to several endangered species, such as the American Crocodile, Indigo Snake, and the Schaus Swallowtail Butterfly.

*It has the world's largest artificial reef.

*Key Largo has a tropical climate. Frost has never been recorded as occurring in Key Largo. In the last decade, the coldest recorded temperature was 34∘F back in 2010.

FYI: In 2016, Marriott Playa Largo Resort opened with the honor of being the first new hotel built in Key Largo in more than two decades! Guests can choose to stay in its three-bedroom beach house, bungalows, or guest rooms. www.playalargoresort.com. But if you want something that's quaint and classic Keys, check out Kona Kai Resort & Botanical Gardens. www.konakairesort.com.

Highlights:

John Pennekamp Coral Reef State Park, Dagny Johnson Key Largo Hammock Botanical State Park, Florida National Marine Sanctuary, Harry Harris Park, swimming with dolphins, scuba diving, *African Queen*, Key Largo Community Park (including YMCA), and Jules Undersea Lodge

For a complete list of outfitters:

www.keylargochamber.org

www.fla-keys.com/keylargo

Islamorada

The name Islamorada means "purple isles" in Spanish. It is not known why Spanish explorers gave that name to these islands. Islamorada became "Islamorada, Village of Islands" when it was incorporated in the late 1990s. It is made up of six islands: Indian Key, Lignumvitae Key, Windley Key, Plantation Key, Lower Matecumbe Key and Upper Matecumbe Key. It is also known as "The Matecumbes."

If you're into fishing, this is the Florida Keys destination for you. It is known as the "Sport Fishing Capital of the World." A saltwater fishing license is required for non-residents if fishing on your own. If you go on a charter boat, you do not need a license. According to Florida Keys Tourism, Florida Bay is home to five of the most sought-after game fish among recreational anglers: bonefish, tarpon, permit, redfish (red drum) and snook. Off the Keys lies the Atlantic Ocean. In these deep-sea areas are some of the greatest sport fish in the world: blue and white marlin, sailfish and swordfish. For more about licenses including how to obtain one http://www.myfwc.com/license/recreational/saltwater-fishing/.

FYI: There are more than 225 species of gamefish in the Keys. If you go offshore in the Gulf, Mahi-Mahi, Tuna, Wahoo, Marlin, Sailfish, Yellowtail, Mangrove Snapper and Mackerel abound in these waters. The Florida Bay is where you'll find Tarpon, Permit, Bonefish, Redfish, Pompano, Shark and Trout. www.fla-keys.com/fishing

While there were Spanish explorers and Native Americans here from at least the 1500s, we don't have much documentation until the 1800s.

It was a small population of hardy folks who lived on the Upper Keys at that time. Conditions were harsh and they were cut off from the mainland until the Overseas Railroad and Overseas Highway arrived in the 1900s. And then John Jacob Houseman arrived on Indian Key. More or less run out of Key West for encroaching on their wrecking business, he moved up to Indian Key and set up shop. While he was not a nice person, he was a successful businessman. He did so well for himself that he soon bought Indian Key.

This became a thriving, bustling community complete with a general store, post office, warehouses, hotel, inn, town square, wharves, and cottages. Things were good until Houseman ran afoul of the law and proposed to capture and kill local Native Americans. It is theorized that they learned of his devious plans and went on the offensive. Indians attacked and destroyed Indian Key in 1840. Houseman and his wife barely escaped with their lives but were forced to leave everything behind. (Houseman was killed in a wrecking accident less than one year later). Others were not so fortunate. While most survived by hiding, eighteen lives were lost during this Seminole raid.

It was a Navy base for a while. At one time there was a Navy hospital, barracks, and outbuildings on Indian Key. There was a malaria epidemic during which time more than four dozen Navy personnel died. The big hurricane of 1935 also killed many island inhabitants, as well as many other folks along the keys. Visitors will see a Hurricane Monument at MM 82, which was erected to remember all those who perished during this natural disaster.

This key was briefly used as a

shipyard. Today, it is known as a tourist destination. In fact, Indian Key is part of the Florida State Park system. You can only get to Indian Key and Lignumvitae Key by boat. The biggest attraction on Lignumvitae is Lignumvitae Key State Botanical Site where visitors will delight in its flora and fauna, such as Mexican Sisals and tamarind groves. www.lignumvitaekey.com. But as is the case with all of the Florida Keys, it is advisable to bring bug spray if you visit.

FYI: The highest elevation in the Keys is Lignumvitae Botanical Site, which is eighteen feet.

History & Discovery Center shares the history of the Florida Keys including the big hurricane of 1935 and the Henry Flagler Railroad. Children 13 and under get in free. www.keysdiscovery.com. MM 82 at Islander Resort.

History of Diving Museum has exhibits and information detailing the history of diving in the Florida Keys. It is amazing to see how diving suits and apparatus, especially helmets, have changed over the years! MM 82.9. www.divingmuseum.org.

Islamorada County Park is a small, but lovely park. It is one of the few places in this area that has a large playground and picnic area. MM 81.5. www.islamorada.fl.us.

Islamorada Founders Park is much larger, encompassing forty acres. This former pineapple plantation is now a waterfront park complete with a skate park, tennis court, heated pool, dog play area, amphitheater, and more. There is an entrance fee but if you're staying on Islamorada you can access the park for free. MM 87. www.islamorada.fl.us/founders_park

Theater of the Sea is the second oldest marine mammal facility in the world. Visitors can see shows and have close up encounters during a glass-bottomed boat ride with sea lions, sea turtles, bottlenose dolphins, stingrays, and sharks. There is also a 17-acre mangrove forest and sanctuary for tropical birds, lizards, and crocodilians. They also have swimming with dolphins and an on-site restaurant, as well as a lagoon beach, snorkeling cruise, and more. Open every day year-round. www.theaterofthesea.com. MM 84.5

Windley Key Fossil Reef State Geologic Site is a thirty-acre park that is open every day except Tuesday and Wednesday. There is an education center and guided tours. MM 85.3. www.floridastateparks.org/windleykey/

FYI: There are several big fishing tournaments held from Jan – July throughout the Keys. These include Islamorada Winter Classic, Marathon International Bonefish Tournament, Jimmy Johnson's National Billfish Championship, Gold Cup Tarpon Tournament, and Drambuie Key West Marlin Tournament. For more about them visit www.fla-keys.com/fishing and www.keysfishingtournaments.com.

If you'd like to arrange for a fishing charter (or guide or boat rental) or do some diving, you can get an up-to-date list of options from www.islamoradachamber.com. Some popular dining and lodging options include **Mangrove Mike's** for breakfast (www.mangrovemikes.com), The **Hungry Tarpon** for seafood (www.hungrytarpon.com), **Lorelei Restaurant and Cabana Bar** for happy hour (www.loreleicabanabar.com), **Pelican Cove Resort** is great for families, (www.pcove.com), **Postcard Inn** for those who want an authentic experience (www.holidayisle.com), and **Green Turtle Cay Inn**, which has a full service bar and restaurant (www.greenturtlekeys.com).

Noteworthy annual events include **Uncorked: Key Largo & Islamorada Food & Wine Festival, Florida Keys Island Fest**, and **Pops in the Park.**

Highlights:

Theater of the Sea, History & Discovery Center, Islamorada County Park, History of Diving Museum, Islamorada Founders Park, and Windley Key Fossil State Geologic Site.

www.islamoradachamber.com

www.fla-keys.com/islamorada

Where should you stay in the Upper Keys?

There are some great places to stay in the Upper Keys, such as Kon Tiki Resort (Islamorada), Cheeca Lodge (Islamorada), Coral Bay Resort (Islamorada), Kona Kai Resort & Botanical Gardens (Key Largo), and Holiday Inn Resort (Key Largo). For a complete list, visit http://visitkeywestonline.com/upstay.htm

Additionally, there are lots of camping options in the Upper Keys:

John Pennekamp Coral Reef State Park, www.floridastateparks.org/pennekamp

Key Largo Campground, www.keylargokampground.com

Calusa Campground Resort &
Marina,
www.calusacampground.com

Blue Fin Rock Harbor Marina &
RV Resort,
www.milemarker97.com

TERRANCE ZEPKE

MIDDLE KEYS

The biggest community in the
Middle Keys is **Marathon**, which
wasn't even incorporated until
1999. Within its city limits are
Boot Key, Knight's Key, Hog Key,
Vaca Key, Stirrup Key, Crawl
Key, Little Crawl Key, East and
West Sister's Island, Deer Key, Fat
Deer Key (excluding the portion in
Key Colony Beach), Long Point
Key, and Grassy Key.

According to legend, Marathon
got its name from railroad
workers. The men who were
employed to complete the Henry
Flagler Railroad worked seven
days a week and up to twelve
hours a day. They sometimes
complained, "This is getting to be
a real marathon." Other sources
credit New York playwright Witter
Bynner with the name Marathon.
Like much of the Keys, Marathon
began as a fishing and farming

community that grew as the wrecking (salvaging) industry grew.

Today, this laid back community boasts the largest live-aboard population on the East Coast. Roughly 100 - 300 boaters live on their vessels year round here.

Marathon is actually a community on Vaca Key. There aren't a lot of attractions here, which the locals like just fine. It does have something that most places along the Keys don't have and that is an 18-hole championship golf course (private), as well as a 9-hole public golf course.

One plus to staying in Marathon is that it offers the cheapest lodging and dining options. What's more, it is centrally-located for visiting other areas of the Keys. You are less than one hour from Key West or

Key Largo, but it could take longer
in peak season.

What can be confusing about
the Keys is their division.
According to the resource, you
will see different listings on maps
and tourism resources for the same
places. I have used the State of
Florida's MM and Keys maps as
my references. According to which
reference you use, the Middle
Keys include Long Key, Conch
Key, Walker Key, Duck Key,
Grassy Key, Crawl Key, Deer
Key, Colony Key, Vaca Key,
Stirrup Key, Boot Key, and Pigeon
Key.

Vaca Key was settled in the
1800s by Bahamians, who grew
produce such as limes, avocados,
and apples. Sea Island cotton was
also grown here. During the early
1800s, this was one of three
wrecking ports in the Keys.

The Indian Key Massacre occurred in 1840, which greatly diminished the population. Most folks fled to Key West and other islands. By the time the Civil War ended, the population was less than five.

What turned things around was the arrival of the Overseas Railroad. Vaca Key became a central base during the time of construction. By the early 1900s, the population had grown to more than 600. The railroad workers renamed it "Marathon."

The Middle Keys grew during this time. Hotels were built, cottages sprang up, streets were paved, and wooden sidewalks were constructed. A major railroad depot opened on Marathon.

Sadly, once the railroad was completed, the population dwindled once again. The remaining population was mostly tied to the fishing industry.

A huge hurricane hit in 1935, wiping out the railroad. The Overseas Highway was completed a few years later and the Keys became a big tourist destination.

All the Middle Keys were farming and fishing communities. Coconuts were grown on Long Key. The Long Key Fishing Club had many prominent members, including baseball legend Ted Williams, Actor/Comedian Jackie Gleason, President Jimmy Carter, and Actor Mike Douglas.

There are some nice beaches that are free and open to the public, including Sombrero (MM 50) and Coco Plum (MM 54). The best bike paths are also at these beaches, as well as Key Colony Beach (MM 53.5) and Marathon Bike Path (MM 47). There are places nearby to rent bikes, canoes, snorkeling gear, and more.

There are golf courses at Key Colony Beach (www.keycolonybeachgolf.com) and Florida Keys Country Club (www.floridakeyscc.com).

Where should you stay in the Middle Keys?

There are some good resorts, such as Buccaneer Resort (Marathon), Grassy Key Beach Resort (Grassy Key) and Best Western Marathon Resort & Marina. For a complete list visit http://visitkeywestonline.com/midstay.htm.

Additionally, you can go camping:

Long Key State Park, www.floridastateparks.org/longkey

Three Fun Facts about Marathon

*It is home to Fisherman's Hospital, which is one of only three hospitals in the Florida Keys & it has the only turtle hospital in the Keys, which is the only state-certified veterinary hospital in the world for sea turtles.

*The tallest building in the Keys, Bonefish Tower (143 feet) is in Marathon.

*The only country club in the Keys, Sombrero Country Club, is here.

FYI: If you're wondering where Henry Flagler got all the money to build this railroad, he was a founding partner in a little enterprise known as Standard Oil Company. His partner was John D. Rockefeller. Did you know that during their lifetime there were NO income taxes in the U.S.? Flagler and

Rockefeller quickly became very rich men. The Overseas Railroad was not his first railroad. That was the Florida East Coast Railroad. Despite its success, many referred to Flagler's vision for a railroad that extended to Key West as "Flagler's Folly." The railroad was completed on January 22, 1912.

Aviation Museum is at Marathon Airport. Open daily, it features a flight simulator, artifacts, photographs, and memorabilia. There is a hanger behind the small museum that houses a DC-3 and a WWII Beechcraft Model 18 cargo plane. Visitors may sit in the aircraft. Free. MM 52.www.fla-keys.com/marathon/marathon_airport.cfm.

FYI: There are two airports in the Keys. One is in Key West and the other is in Marathon at MM 52, which is roughly the center of the Keys. The airport services privately owned, corporate and charter aircraft. Rental cars and taxi service are available.

Crane Point Hammock is a 64-acre botanical preserve. There is also The Museum & Nature Center of Crane Point, which includes a Museum of Natural History, Marathon Wild Bird Center, and a Children's Center with all kinds of cool stuff including a touch tank and pirate ship. Self-guided walks can be achieved along any of the nature trails and the saltwater lagoon that includes plaques explaining flora and fauna. There are many birds, butterflies, and exotic plants, as well as rare animals and plant species. There is also the Adderly Town Historic Site. There is a fee for everyone except ages four and under. MM 50. www.cranepoint.net.

Curry Hammock State Park
extends 600 acres. It remains
undeveloped and unspoiled, so it is a
great place to experience the Keys.
Visitors can hike, kayak, canoe,
picnic, and relax. MM 55.
www.floridastateparks.org/curryham
mock/default.cfm.

Dolphin Research Center educates
and entertains all ages with an
opportunity to interact with sea lions
and dolphins. Grassy Key.
http://www.dolphins.org/.

Florida Keys Country Club offers golf and tennis. The 139-acre club is open to the public. 4000 Sombrero Boulevard.
http://www.floridakeyscc.com/.

Hawks Cay Resort is the biggest resort in the Keys. It has restaurants, bars, pools, lagoons, marina, spa and fitness center, and a dolphin encounter area. Guests may select from a wide variety of resort programs (such as a magic show and mermaid school) and activities, including tennis, diving, kiteboarding, paddle surfing, fishing charters, watersports, and three different dolphin programs. 61 Hawks Cay Boulevard, Duck Key.
www.hawkscay.com.

Key Colony Beach Golf Course is open to the public. It is a par three 9-hole course. 460 8th Street, Key Colony Beach.

Long Key State Park includes a beach, boardwalk, nature trails, camping, restrooms/showers, large picnic/grill area, lagoon, and wildlife watching. There are lots of shorebirds and marine life that can be observed. You may even spot the elusive Key West Quail Dove here. Snorkeling is permitted, canoes and bikes can be rented, and there are ranger programs seasonally. The Long Key State Recreation Area extends nearly 1,000 acres. There are two fees to enter: a per person fee and a vehicle fee but it is nominal. Long Key was once the site of Henry Flagler's fishing camp and a stop on his railroad. Both were destroyed by the famous Labor Day hurricane of 1935. But visitors can camp into the Long Key State Park, which has a full-service campground.

MM 67.5.
https://www.floridastateparks.org/par
k/Long-Key

Museum of Natural History & Children's Museum offers touch tanks, tropical fish feeding, exhibits, and a nature trail.

Old Seven Mile Bridge was replaced by a state-of-the-art Seven Mile Bridge in 1982. The old bridge was never torn down because to do so is cost prohibitive. Plus, many old timers find comfort in seeing it. Walkers, bikers, and joggers still utilize it. The first two miles of the bridge serve as a recreational site.

Pigeon Key is connected to the mainland by the Old Seven Mile Bridge. The three-acre key sits just five feet above sea level. It is a park that includes Pigeon Key Village. The village is comprised of historic buildings, a museum, and an education center. This park is open to the public for a fee, which includes a ferry ticket from Knight's Key to Pigeon Key. There is good snorkeling here, as well as a nice picnic area. The Pigeon Key Art Festival is held every February. This key can be accessed by foot via the Seven Mile Bridge or by ferry service. Pigeon Key Visitor's Center & Gift Shop is on Knight's Key, MM 47. www.pigeonkey.net.

FYI: There are seven species of sea turtles found worldwide and five of these turtles can be found in the Florida Keys: Loggerhead, Hawksbill, Leatherback, Kemps Ridley, and Green Sea Turtle.

Turtle Hospital was established in 1986. It rescues injured sea turtles and rehabilitates them, ultimately returning them to the wild if possible. They have their own ambulance and vet staff! Guided tours are offered. A fee is charged that goes toward the

cost of saving these sea turtles. MM
48.5. www.turtlehospital.org.

*FYI: The Florida Keys is the first region in
North America to offer "Jetpack
Experiences." Participants strap on a
JetLev R200 flight pack and a 30-foot hose
tethers the apparatus to a tiny boat with a
pump that uses seawater as propellant.
Flight controls allow individuals to take off,
.make soft turns, hover and land as the boat
is dragged behind. Wow!*

Veteran's Memorial Park and Beach is popular with daytrippers. There is a nice little beach, picnic area, and boat ramp. There are no restrooms/showers or other amenities. FREE. Open daily. MM 40.

Highlights:

Aviation Museum, Crane Point Museum, Curry Hammock State Park, Museum of Natural History & Children's Museum, Old Seven Mile Bridge, Long Key State Park, Pigeon Key, Turtle Hospital, and Veteran's Memorial Park & Beach.

www.fla-keys.com/marathon

TERRANCE ZEPKE

LOWER KEYS

Lower Keys

*Author Note: Even though Key West is a
part of the Lower Keys, I'm going to discuss
it in a separate chapter.*

The Lower Keys extend for
approximately thirty-three miles.
Much of this area is residential and
does not have much of interest to
tourists. There are only a few shops
and restaurants. There is a big flea
market open on the weekends
(www.floridakeysfleamarket.com).
   The biggest thing in the Lower
Keys is **Boca Chica Naval Air
Station** (MM 7). It was established
because here because this area has the
most "perfect flying days" of
anywhere in America.
   There is a small private airport
at Sugarloaf Key where **aerial tours
and skydiving** can be arranged.
   **Loe Key National Marine
Sanctuary** is less than five miles

from Big Pine Key and offers good diving and snorkeling. An *underwater* concert is held here every July.

FYI: Looe Key Sanctuary is a great diving spot. The reef is named after the HMS Looe, a British frigate that sunk here. The five-mile sanctuary was established in 1975. Up to 150 fish species and 50 species of coral can be found here.

Bahia Honda State Park dock is the departure place for Looe Key snorkeling trips. Snorkeling gear can be rented, as well as kayaks, paddles, wetsuits, and life jackets. Additionally, beach supplies, such as chairs and umbrellas, can be rented. Snacks and sunscreen can be bought, as well. Camping is permitted at the Bahia Honda State Park and there are also cabins available. To rent either contact Reserve America at 800-326-3521. www.bahiahondapark.com. MM 38.

FYI: Florida Keys camping will expose you to the elements. You may encounter sweltering heat, a thunderstorm, no see-ums or mosquitoes, and intense sun all in the same day! Make sure you are prepared for inclement weather, have plenty of water, bug spray, food (and ice for perishables), and extra clothing. Wear a wide-brimmed hat and UV sunglasses.

Arguably, the best camping in the Keys is in the Lower Keys:

Bahia Honda State Park, www.floridastateparks.org/bahiahonda

Bluewater Key RV Resort, www.bluewaterkey.com

Boyd's Key West Campground, www.boydscampground.com

Fort Jefferson in the Dry Tortugas http://www.florida-keys-guide.com/dry-tortugas-national-park/

Geiger Key Marina,
www.geigerkeymarina.com

Lazy Lakes Campground & RV
Resort, www.lazylakeresort.com

Leo's Campground & RV Park,
www.leoscampground.com

Sunshine Key RV Resort &
Marina, www.rvonthego.com

Sugarloaf Key Resort KOA
Kampground,
www.thefloridakeys.com/koasugar
loaf

For more lodging options visit
http://visitkeywestonline.com/stay.ht
m

*FYI: In addition to many ads,
documentaries, specials, and television
series filmed here, many movies have*

been shot in the Keys, such as True Lies, Red Dragon, 2 Fast 2 Furious, Key Largo, Miami Vice, Meet the Fockers, Tomorrow Never Dies, Speed 2, Office Space, Heartbreakers, Up Close and Personal, License to Kill, and Repo Man.

Bat Tower is one of the most unusual tourist attractions. Around the 1920's, Richter Perky attempted to establish a fishing camp on Sugarloaf Key. The mosquitoes in the area were so bad that he decided to build a bat tower. But things didn't go according to his plan. The bats were not interested in the mosquitoes. The tower still stands in hopes that one day soon the bats may change their minds. MM 17.

Big Pine Key Community Park is a nice park where visitors can picnic and relax after a long drive down US 1. MM 31.

Florida Keys National Wildlife Refuges Visitor Center has free information and wildlife exhibits. Big Pine Key Plaza on Key Deer Boulevard. MM30.

National Deer Key & Great Heron Refuge was established to protect the deer population, which is most unique. What makes these animals different from other deer is their size. Dubbed the "toy deer" the Key Deer is only about two feet tall. They weigh between 65 – 85 pounds. Their coloring is different too. It is a reddish brown or a slate gray. From a distance, a Key Deer can be mistaken for a dog.

The Key Deer is a sub-species of the Virginia white-tailed deer. It cannot be found anywhere else in the world. It is thought that they came to the Keys from the mainland across a long land bridge from 6,000 to 12,000 years ago when the Wisconsin Glacier melted. The waters rose and divided this land bridge into the islands of the Florida Keys.

You will often see them along the Overseas Highway as you approach Big Pine Key and at No Name Key.

In addition to these cute, little deer, the 9,000-acre refuge is home to many other animals, including turtles, alligators, fish, and wading birds, such as the Great White Heron.

Also located within this refuge is the Blue Hole, which is the largest body of freshwater in the Keys. There is an observation deck and you'll often find a naturalist on hand. The Key Deer Refuge office is a good place to start. MM 30 at Big Pine Shopping Center. www.fws.gov/nationalkeydeer

FYI: Deer are most active in the early morning and at night, beginning in the early evening. But they are spotted at all times during the day. The best way to

view them is to stay in your vehicle. Do not approach them on foot, extend your arms out towards them, hang out the window, or shout at them. Be sure to respect the slow speed limit as you will get a ticket if you exceed the speed limit.

Fat Albert is a big, white blimp that hovers over Cudjoe Key. It is helping to guard or protect the Keys from an aerial vantage point. So be sure to look up as you go through the Lower Keys.

No Name Pub is a long-time icon that is two miles off U.S. 1 at Big Pine Key. It is renowned for its pizza and for being a bit tricky to find. It is the oldest bar in the Lower Keys. The No

Name Pub has been a bait shop, general store, and brothel. But it has been the No Name Pub since the 1950s.

Sugarloaf Key and its Sugarloaf Lodge is the place to go for an authentic Keys experience. The classic Keys lodge has is 31 rooms and its own airstrip. MM 17. The family-owned lodge is inside the Great White Heron Refuge. It has everything you need for a perfect Keys holiday—a marina, bike rentals, bait shop, kayak rentals, fishing charters, restaurant, skydiving, swimming pool, and tiki bar. Additionally, they offer all kinds of classes and special activities, such as yoga, painting, and a guided walk to the Bat Tower.
www.sugarloaflodge.net.

FYI: The best thing about the Keys is the great outdoors but along with this comes insects. There are more than 40 species of mosquitoes in the Keys. Most are but not harmful but a few do carry disease that can be transmitted if bitten by an infected bug. Monroe County does have a regular spraying schedule but wearing insect repellent is advisable at all times.

For information about area B&Bs, guest cottages, and motels, contact www.lowerkeyschamber.com to get an up-to-date list and be sure to check out http://www.visitthekeys.com/best-places, www.booking.com/florida-keys, http://www.floridakeys.com/lowerkeys/lower-keys-accommodations.htm

*FYI: Want to know a well-kept secret?
There is a resort on the Lower Keys.
Little Palm Island Resort is located on
Munson Island. This lovely retreat is
accessible by boat or seaplane only.
Once on the island, guests are shown to
their cottages on stilts, which come with
secluded sun decks, mini-bars, Jacuzzis,
ceiling fans, and hammocks. Visitors are
permitted to come over for lunch or
dinner on a free ferry that departs from
MM 28.5 but reservations are required.
Be prepared! Whether you're dining or
staying at Little Palm, it won't be cheap.
But visitors are rewarded with lots of
privacy, pampering, and palms.*

Highlights:

Boca Chica Naval Air Station, Key Deer, Loe Key National Marine Sanctuary, Bahia Honda State Park, Big Pine Community Park, Florida Keys Wildlife Refuge Visitor's Center, National Deer & Great Heron Refuge, Bat Tower, Fat Albert, No Name Pub and Sugarloaf Lodge.

For a complete list of companies and outfitters that offer kayaking tours, nature tours, boat and bike rentals, diving, snorkeling, ultralight airplane rides, skydiving and more, contact

www.lowerkeyschamber.com

FYI: GREAT FREEBIE!
Send a free e-postcard featuring
the highlights of the Florida
Keys. Choose from several
beautiful cards at
http://www.floridakeys.com/post
cards/

TERRANCE ZEPKE

KEY WEST

Key West

Key West is the crown jewel of the
Florida Keys. In fact, some folks
choose to fly into Key West
International Airport and spend time
exclusively in Key West without
seeing any other Keys. I think you're
missing a lot if you choose to do that
but if your time and budget are
limited then that is an option. You
should know that it is not cheap to fly
into Key West so you may do better
to fly into Miami or Fort Lauderdale
and drive the Overseas Highway. I
think the only time I would
recommend flying rather than driving
would be for those short on time.
http://www.keywestinternationalairpo
rt.com/ and www.fla-
keys.com/gettinghere

Key West is documented on maps as
Cayo Hueso (Bone Key) as far back

as the early 1600s. This sounds about right given that Florida was discovered by a Spanish explorer, Ponce de Leon, in 1513.

It got its name from early explorers who found human bones all over the beach when they came ashore. They were mostly likely the remains of Calusa Indians, who fought a bloody battle here against another Indian tribe. The Calusas had been pushed all the way down the coast to Key West where they had no choice but to stand their ground and fight or die. Most perished during this attack but some made it to Cuba, which is roughly ninety miles away.

The Spanish Crown gave Key West to Juan Pablo Salas in 1815. Salas sold it to John Simonton, who had great plans for this land. He divided it into parcels and sold them to three other businessmen.

At some point, the name was changed from Cayo Hueso to Key West, presumably because the Bone

Key was not a good name for a place you're trying to develop.

Today you will notice that many of the streets in Key West are named after these prominent businessmen, including Simonton, Fleming, and Whitehead.

By the early 1800s, a naval presence known as the Mosquito Fleet was established to deter piracy and slave trading.

By 1828, Key West was incorporated and growing by leaps and bounds. Sponging, cigar making, fishing/turtling, salt, and wrecking/salvaging became big business.

For more than three decades, Key West was the biggest producer of salt in America. This was a big deal because salt was the best preservative of food until refrigeration was invented. That ended when a hurricane destroyed the salt tidal pools. But that didn't slow down the local economy one bit. In fact, Key West was the richest city, per capita, of anywhere in the U.S. by the mid-1800s. It also had a big population—nearly 3,000 by that time.

These were the glory days of wrecking/salvaging. Things were good in the Keys until the era of lighthouses and lightships. Once these navigational aids were established, there were fewer shipwrecks and therefore less salvaging of fine silks and linens, rum, wine, silverware, furniture, lace, and leather goods.

Just like the rest of our country, Key West was affected by the Civil War, which began in 1861. Fort Taylor was a key fort and the East Coast Blockade Squadron was assigned to stop blockade runners from getting through the Gulf of Mexico. Key West had a big impact on the outcome of the war. The East Coast Blockade Squadron prevented more than 300 ships from getting supplies through to Confederate troops who desperately needed them. The Union seized all the cargo and impounded every last one of these ships.

Many Cubans fled to Key West when the Cuban Revolution began in 1868. Many got jobs in the cigar industry, which was bringing close to one million dollars into Key West a year. In its heyday, there were roughly 130 cigar factories in Key West and production exceeded 100,000 cigars a year. The industry was dead by the turn of the century. Most manufacturers left Key West to relocate where there was no union, and more incentives, such as no taxes and a cheaper labor force.

The end of the sponging industry came in the early 1900s. It went from well over 1,000 men being employed to nearly none. Again, incentives played a big part of the demise. Key West was remote whereas Tampa and Tarpon Springs were not. A fungus killed all the sponge beds in the state. It has taken more than two decades for sponge beds to reproduce. Today, sponging is again an industry, albeit it on a much smaller scale than before when more than 150 tons of sponge were being harvested a year.

All these industries were soon replaced with a new one—tourism. When the Overseas Railroad was completed in 1912, visitors were finally able to easily get from the mainland to Key West. At a cost of $25 million and 600-700 lives lost, the railroad made Key West a viable vacation spot until a hurricane annihilated it less than twenty-five years later. But it is as if fate will always smile down on Key West. The Overseas Highway opened in 1938. Now there was no stopping tourism and smuggling.

Key West became an important

place during Prohibition. Ships brought booze from the Bahamas and Cuba to Key West and beyond. It is said that some of the finest, most distinguished families made their money or at least part of their fortunes bootlegging.

Most of the residents of Key West were receiving some kind of relief during the Great Depression, except for the bootleggers.

What turned things around economically for Key West and much of America was World War II. The Navy established a base and put 25,000 sailors in Key West. Key West was known as a military town until the submarine base close in the mid-1970s.

Things were bad for a while after that but tourism became the new big thing. Key West built attractions and capitalized on its natural attractions to lure tourists. Thousands of tourists flocked to the island hamlet each year. By the millennium, that number has reached the millions.

What draws us to Key West? What makes Key West so unique?

The vibe, for one thing. You feel relaxed and breathe easier and deeper as soon as you arrive. I attribute that to the ambiance. There are colorful conch houses that feature a combination of architectural designs, including Queen Anne, Bahamian, Revival, Eyebrow, and Shotgun.

Visitors also enjoy the tropical climate and laid back attitude. It seems no one is in a hurry here. Stress is an unknown (or dirty) word. Clothing is casual (or optional in some establishments!). The food is good and often a clever infusion of Caribbean and Floridian cuisine. Drinks are frothy and tasty with creative names that cry out to be ordered, such as Sunset Coladas and Key Lime Martinis.

So how did the Keys get the nickname 'Conch Republic'? The story dates back to April 23, 1982. This is the day that the Florida Keys seceded from the United States. This is the first time a secession has occurred since the Civil War.

On April 18, U.S. Border & Customs Patrol set up unannounced blockades on U.S. 1 at Florida City, which is just north of the Keys and the only road to and from the Keys. The roadblocks meant that each and every vehicle had to prove that everyone in the vehicle was a U.S. citizen. Plus, every vehicle was subject to be searched since the Border Patrol was looking for illegals and drugs. You can imagine the traffic gridlocks this caused. We're talking up to twenty miles of backed-up traffic. Not only was this inconvenient for locals, it was very bad for tourism.

Folks didn't take kindly to this

given that this was taking place more than one hundred miles from any border. When no relief was found using the U.S. court system, Key West Mayor Dennis Wardlow informed the media that "Tomorrow at noon the Florida Keys will secede from the Union!"

As promised, at noon the next day, the mayor read his secession proclamation. The media listened as he announced that the Conch Republic was now an independent nation—no longer a part of America.

The secession activities included lowering the U.S. flag and raising the Conch Republic flag, naming new officials (such as Secretary of Underwater Affairs and Minister of Nutrition) and his breaking a loaf of stale Cuban bread over the head of a man dressed as a U.S. Navy officer. Following this short rebellion ceremony, the mayor wrapped up by surrendering to the Admiral of the local navy base while also requesting a billion dollars in aid money!

The succession was short-lived and the reparation money was never received, but the media attention brought the end of the roadblocks, so all's well that ends well. Conch Republic Independence Day is still celebrated every April throughout the Keys. You will see t-shirts and bumper stickers for sale all over the place that refer to this historical moment, *"We Seceded Where Others Failed."* You can even buy a souvenir passport.

The Conch Republic does not refer to Key West but to all of the Keys, although Key West was designated as its capital. All the land north of Key West was called Northern Territories.

FYI: While there is little negative to say about Key West, one can complain about the parking. There are only a few pay lots and limited street parking, which is expensive when you can find it. And don't get excited if you see a space on a side street as parking on side streets is for locals only. You will be towed. It is best to stay at a hotel or rental with parking included and don't move your car. Taxis, bikes, and scooters/mopeds are available for rent and the best way to get around. Or look for Park N' Ride signs, such as Old Town Park N' Ride Parking Garage at Carolina & Grinnel Streets, which includes free public transportation (www.ketransit.com). For those honeymooning in Key West or celebrating some other special occasion, there is limo service. Southernmost Limos offers airport transfers and hourly or daily rentals.
www.southernmostlimos.com.

Where Should You Stay in Key West?

Accommodations vary greatly in Key West, from gay guesthouses to green (eco-friendly) lodging. There is a wide range of options to suit any traveler's wish list. You'll find camping/RV sites, motels, inns, vacation rentals and more. Best upscale lodging: Westin Key West Resort & Marina, Cypress House Hotel, Ocean Key Resort & Spa, Hyatt Key West Resort & Spa, Waldorf Astoria Casa Marina Resort, Weatherstation Inn, and Marriot Beachside Key West Hotel Resort.

It is a challenge to find cheap lodging in Key West. The best deals will be on vacation rentals or specials through sites like AirBnB.com, Priceline.com or Booking.com. Also, look for seasonal specials and discounted packages on resort websites. AAA, AARP, military and government employees receive discounted rates at most places. You should be able to negotiate a better rate than what you see advertised by calling the property directly, especially if it is not peak season.

For more about Key West lodging: www.keywestinns.com, http://www.fla-keys.com/propsearch/accomloc.cfm

www.keywestinfo.com and www.vacationhomesofkeywest.com.

If you don't have any budget restrictions, Sunset Key Resort offers cottages on a private 27-acre island that is just minutes from Key West. It has a restaurant, pool, bar, and spa. www.sunsetkeycottages.com.

Another option is to rent a cottage.
Many residents have built cute
cottages behind their homes that
can be rented out by Century 21
Keysearch Realty
(www.c21search.com), Rent Key
West (www.rentkeywest.com), and
Preferred Properties Coastal Realty
(www.realkeywest.com). The best
rates will be weekly rather than
nightly and during the low or off
season as opposed to the high
season. These vary greatly in cost
and amenities so take some time

researching before you book to
make sure you get what you want.

*FYI: Writers who
are or were inspired by living in Key
West include Judy Blume (one of my
favorite authors), Robert Frost, Tom
Corcoran, John Leslie, John Hersey,
Wallace Stevens, Nancy Friday, Richard
Wilbur, Tennessee Williams, and Ernest
Hemingway. There are a great many
fiction books set in the Keys and
nonfiction books about the Keys. Do a
Google or Amazon search to discover
some great books, such as Papa
Hemingway in Key West, To Have and
Have Not, Cookin' in the Keys, and Blue
Moon.*

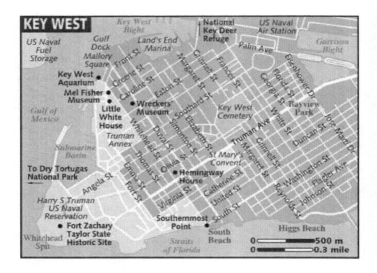

Key West Attractions

Audubon House & Tropical Gardens was formerly home to the first harbor pilot in Key West, Captain John Geiger. While it's a great example of 19-th century Keys architecture, its main appeal is its gardens. Visitors will find orchids, bromeliads, banana trees, herb garden, nursery, and a nice gift shop. 205

Whitehead Street. Kids under 6 are free. Open daily until 4:30 p.m. www.audubonhouse.com

Curry Mansion is a five-story Victorian mansion that dates back to 1905. Self-guided tours are available until 5 p.m. 511 Carolina Street.

Custom House Museum is a good place to go to learn more about the colorful history of Key West. Children 6 and under are admitted free. Open daily until 4:30 p.m. 281 Front Street. www.kwahs.org.

Dry Tortugas National Park is located seventy miles from Key West. Visitors are transported aboard the ferry, *Yankee Freedom*. Upon arrival, visitors have lots of options: swimming, snorkeling, scuba diving, sunbathing, bird watching, and tours of Fort Jefferson. The unfinished fortress consists of cells, cannons, and a moat. The only other way to reach this archipelago of seven islands is by seaplane. There is a nominal fee to enter the park. www.drytortugas.com.

FYI: Dry Tortugas National Park is located on 16-acre Garden Key. It includes Fort Jefferson, which is the largest masonry structure in the Western Hemisphere— taking up more than ten acres—and is composed of more than 16 million bricks. Construction began in 1846 but was never completed. The Dry Tortugas are known as having some of the best snorkeling anywhere in the Lower Keys. The Tortugas are also known for their bird population. Up to 200 different species of birds can be seen here so bring your camera and binoculars. The best birding months are March – September. Camping is permitted and is an incredible experience here but there are limited sites so be sure to make a reservation as soon you possible. https://www.drytortugasinfo.com/.

East Martello Museum & Gardens is one of the stops on the Ghosts & Graveyards Tour because of Robert the Doll (see next page). There are lots of exhibits chronicling Key West history and a great art gallery. Exhibits include sponging, cigar making, wrecking, and Cuban Missile Crisis. It is open daily until 4:30 p.m. 3501 S. Roosevelt Boulevard. www.kwahs.org.

West Martello Tower is leased to the Key West Garden Club and is a permanent horticultural (botanical) exhibit. 1100 Atlantic Boulevard. For more about this site and tower history, http://keywestgardenclub.com/Tower_History.htmlhttp://keywestgardenclub.com/Tower_History.html

Beware of ROBERT THE DOLL...

The most famous artifact in the East Martello Museum is Robert the Doll. I first learned about creepy Robert (and scary Annabelle) when reading *The Demonologist* by Ed and Lorraine Warren. That's when I learned that objects can be evil and cursed.

Robert the Doll is a large doll that is dressed as an early 20th-century naval officer. The doll was reportedly given to Gene Otto by a Bahamian servant who was skilled in black magic and may have 'cursed' the doll. Whenever Gene got into trouble he blamed the doll, insisting *"Robert did it!"* Gene kept the doll even after he grew up. In fact, Robert the Doll remained in Gene's possession until his death in 1974.

Over the years, there were all kinds of strange reports from family members, visitors, and workmen. There were reports of footsteps in the attic and a child's laughter. The doll was often found in a different location from where it had been left and a strong energy was repeatedly reported emitting from the doll. When Myrtle Reuter bought the Otto house after Gene's death, she "inherited" the doll.

She kept the doll for six years before
donating it to the East Martello
Museum. She got rid of the doll
because she swore he was moving
around her house on his own. She
kept finding him in a different room
or floor from where she had put him.
Too creepy!

Museum staff swear that strange stuff has happened ever since the doll arrived. Any ghost tour you take in Key West will include a ghost story about Robert the Doll. To watch a short Robert the Doll documentary, http://www.historyvshollywood.com/video/robert-the-doll-documentary/ or for more about the Robert the Doll exhibit go to http://www.kwahs.org/exhibitions/online-exhibitions/robert-the-doll/#sthash.qnyr2U7s.dpuf

FYI: More hauntings & ghosts can be found at other Key West locales, such as Hard Rock Café, Cypress House, Captain Tony's Saloon, Ripley's Believe It or Not Odditorium, and The Chelsea House.

Ernest Hemingway Home and Museum is a must for Key West visitors or maybe that's just how I feel as a fellow writer. But lots of other folks must feel the same way because

I didn't encounter crowds of this size at any other attraction. Not only will you learn about Hemingway and all his wives, you'll also get a tour of the house and grounds, which includes his writing studio (I want it!), pool, gardens, and famous six-toed cats. You'll get a good look at them and lots of chances for photos as the guides keep treats in their pockets and the cats know it. There is a nice gift shop on site and the stories about Hemingway, his great works, and Old Key West are fascinating. You'll also learn why he left and why he never returned. This property is a National Historic Landmark. 907 Whitehead Street. www.hemingwayhome.com.

FYI: In 1935, Ernest Hemingway received a cat named Snowball. With paws featuring six toes, "Snowball" was the first of a long line of felines that help make the Hemingway House Museum one of the most popular visitor attractions in the Florida Keys.

Flagler Station Museum is at the Historic Key West Seaport (corner of Caroline and Margaret Streets). While there you must visit its mercantile store filled with nostalgia and watch a short film about the Overseas Railroad. This museum takes you back in time to when it all began—to the era travel first became possible to the remote reaches of the Florida Keys. www.flaglerstation.net.

Florida Keys Eco-Discovery Center offers interactive exhibits, dioramas, and cool displays highlighting the natural history of the Keys. Visitors can take a virtual dive, see a replica of the world's only underwater ocean lab, enjoy an HD movie about a young adventurer, watch a reef video, and see a 2,400-gallon aquarium featuring a living reef. Closed on Sundays and Mondays and holidays. 35 E. Quay Road (across from the

Fort Zachary Taylor Historic State
Park). FREE.
www.floridakeys.noaa.gov.

**Harry S. Truman Little White
House** is Florida's only Presidential
Museum and is on the National
Register of Historic Places. A tour of
this museum house reveals its rich
history. The house dates back to 1890
so there's a lot of history! President
Truman used the house as both a
retreat and an office. Records show he
was here at least 175 days, so a lot of
presidential business happened here,
including Truman's Civil Rights
Executive Order being enacted from
here. President John F. Kennedy met
with the British Prime Minister at the
Little White House just 23 days
before the infamous Bay of Pigs
incident. U.S. Secretary of State Colin
Powell held peace talks here with the
Armenia and Azerbaijan
governments. You'll learn a good bit
more about this unimposing two-story

wooden building during tours that take place every half hour until 4:30 p.m. 111 Front Street. The admission fee includes a self-guided tour of the botanical garden.
www.trumanlittlewhitehouse.com.

FYI: Pick up brochures at the Key West Chamber of Commerce or visitor's center. Or you can go online to find discounts on most tours and attractions. For example, the Key West Butterfly & Nature Conservancy brochure includes a coupon good for discounted admission.

Key West Aquarium has a touch tank and a half dozen exhibits. To be honest, I was not impressed with this aquarium. In fact, we left within an hour of arriving so as not to waste any more time here. If you been to other aquariums, such as Sea World, Baltimore Aquarium, and Two Worlds Aquarium, you will probably be disappointed because this is much smaller with only a few exhibits and tanks. 1 Whitehead Street. www.keywestaquarium.com.

Key West Butterfly & Nature Conservancy has been voted the #1 attraction in Key West by People's Choice Awards, TripAdvisor, and Yelp. Be advised that this is something you want to do early in the day because it will be easier to tour this 85-degree habitat before you get too hot and sweaty from the Key West humidity. There are close to sixty species of beautiful butterflies, as well as birds, frogs, and flowers. It is open daily until 5:30 but tickets are not sold after 4:30 p.m. 1316 Duval Street. Free to children age 3 or under. www.keywestbutterfly.com.

Key West Cemetery is a 16-acre cemetery with an estimated 100,000 people buried here. This means that more people 'reside' in the cemetery than they do in the town of Key West.

Margaret & Angela Streets. A free
cemetery map and self-guided tour
can be printed out at
http://www.keywesttravelguide.com/k
ey-west-cemetery.

**Key West First Legal Rum
Distillery** is open daily until sunset.
Visitors can take tours and participate
in free rum tastings. There is a gift
shop if you like what you taste! 105
Simonton Street.
www.keywestlegalrum.com.

**Key West Heritage House Museum
and Robert Frost Cottage** (where
Poet Robert Frost spent 16 winters) is
a good example of a traditional conch
house and offers an impressive
collection of fine antiques dating back
several generations. 410 Caroline
Street.
https://www.facebook.com/pages/Key-
West-Heritage-House-Museum-and-Robert-
Frost-Cottage/108085445886386

Key West Lighthouse and Keeper's Quarter's Museum is open daily and can be climbed all the way to the top—88 steps! During the tour, you'll hear stories about this beacon and its keepers. This lighthouse dates back to 1826 and is an island icon. Children under 6 years old are admitted free. 938 Whitehead Street. www.kwahs.org.

Key West Roosters. Here's a listing you won't find in other guidebooks. This is a free and easily accessible attraction since these little fellows are all over the place. Called gypsy chickens by locals, these farm animals freely roam around Key West. I was awakened my first morning by the crowing of several roosters. Given that we were in a port town nowhere near an agricultural area, I initially thought I was having a dream (We arrived in the evening so I didn't see all the hens and roosters). Imagine my surprise to open the door and see them all over the resort parking lot! I later learned that these gypsy chickens are also controversial chickens. Some locals love them and some hate them. Some tourists love them and some hate them. Like them or not, Key West roosters are not going anywhere as far as I can tell so be forewarned. Well, actually, some are being transported to chicken farms (where they will eat, sleep and lay eggs) and other safe havens in an effort to reduce the population. Where did they come from? Some say they date back to when we got our own dinner and some say they were once used in cockfighting. When it became illegal they simply turned them loose. However they got here, they are just another quirky thing about Key West.

Relocated Rooster (Botanic Gardens of Martello Towers, Key West Garden Club)

Key West Shipwreck Museum is a unique experience. Ticket holders gather out front waiting for their cue. It comes loud and clear. *Wreck Ashore!* With these words shouted by a costumed salvager, participants are ushered into the museum and into a different era. The museum uses a combination of artifacts, displays, costumed actors, and video footage to present the colorful maritime history of the Florida Keys, which includes the heyday of the wrecking industry.

The tour concludes with an optional climb up a 65' lookout tower. This affords a great view of Key West. The museum is among my favorite things to do in Key West as it explores such an important era in Key West history and does so in a highly entertaining way. 1 Whitehead Street. www.keywestshipwreck.com.

Key West Tropical Forest & Botanical Garden is an 11-acre collection of thousands of exotic trees, shrubs, butterfly species, plants, and palms. There is also a picnic area and amphitheater. It is open daily for self-guided tours. Free admission for locals on the first Sunday of every month. 5210 College Road, Stock Island. www.keywestbotanicalgarden.org.

Mel Fisher Maritime Museum has all kinds of cool exhibits, including Science of Shipwrecks, Real Pirates of the Caribbean, Key West African Cemetery, and more. See real treasure loot while learning about archeology and conservation. 200 Greene Street. Open every day until 5 p.m. www.melfishermuseum.org.

Ripleys Believe It or Not! Odditorium is on my "highly recommended" list. For about $10, visitors have access to more than 10,000 square feet of exhibits. Good thing they're open until 10 p.m. year round since they have 550 artifacts and exhibits and 15 themed galleries. 108 Duval Street. Note: Ripley's also offers Haunted Lockdown, which is a special after-hours tour of the Odditorium that is allegedly haunted. www.ripley.com/keywest.

Southernmost Point is a huge, concrete buoy, which is a popular place for tourist photos. Be prepared to wait in line unless you come early or late. It is at the junction of South and Whitehead Streets—you can't miss it. Across the street from this southernmost point of the U.S. landmark is a Queen Anne style mansion surrounded by palms. It is known as the Southernmost House.

Wrecker's Museum is the oldest house in Key West, dating back to the 1820s. 322 Duval Street (moved from the intersection of Caroline and Whitehead Streets). Tours are given by volunteers and there are limited hours of operation so be sure to check for the latest schedule. FREE. www.oirf.org.

FYI: There are sunset celebrations nightly at Mallory Square. But you don't have to wait until the sun drops below the yardarm. These celebrations begin a full two hours before sunset to allow ample time to enjoy all the entertainment before darkness falls. This has been a Key West tradition since the 1960s. You don't want to miss this! The entertainers vary but on any given night you will see some combination of musicians, magicians, jugglers, clowns, acrobats, sword swallowers, tightrope walkers, unicyclists, escape artists, balloon artists, animal acts, and psychic readers. Additionally, there are lots of food vendors and an indescribable vibe! For really daring souls, you can partake in "Naked Sunset" at the Garden of Eden, a clothing optional bar at the corner of Duval and Caroline Streets.

Five Things You Should Do:

1. Sample a delightful Florida Keys key lime specialty, such as key lime ice cream or a key lime martini or milkshake or stock up on key lime goodies at **All Things Key Lime** at 200

Elizabeth Street and 802 Duval
Street. www.keylimeshop.com.

2. Have a cold (alcoholic or non-
   alcoholic) drink and listen to
   some good music at iconic
   Sloppy Joe's. Be sure to
   sample their conch fritters and
   be forewarned that it gets loud
   and crowded. 201 Duval Street.
   www.sloppyjoes.com.

3. Enjoy **Sunset Celebration at
   Mallory Square**. Hard to say
   which is better—the sunset or
   the entertainment?

4. Pose for a picture in front of the
   large concrete **Southernmost
   Point** buoy marker. You are
   just 90 miles from Cuba!

5. Take a **conch train tour** that
   shares Key West history and
   trivia or a **ghost tour** of Old
   Town and discover its
   supernatural side. Options

range from ghost walks to haunted trolley tours.

*　　*　　*

FYI: There are lots of nicknames for The Keys and Key West, such as The Rock, The Keys, Paradise, Gibraltar of the West, and the Conch Republic. Key West is known as the Southernmost City in the continental U.S. and the official city motto is "One Human Family."

Key West Tours

Conch Tour Train is a fun way to see Key West. The "engineer" doubles as a tour guide, sharing lots of great trivia. All ages will be entertained. Also, considering the size of Key West, it is one of the best ways to see all of its attractions. The 90-minute tour departs from Front Street Depot and ends at Mallory Square. The train makes a loop through Old Town Key West that includes three stops: Station Depot, Truval Village, and Flagler Station.

The stops last ten minutes during which time passengers may get off the train and use the restroom or shop for souvenirs and refreshments (permitted on the train). Or passengers may get off and explore on their own, picking the train up at a later time or different location. The Conch Tour Train runs every day from 9 a.m. until 4:30 p.m and features 24 places of interest. Children 12 and under ride free and there are senior and military discounts. www.historictours.com.

FYI: The conch train and the trolley tour are comparable in all aspects, including price, sights, and narration. The big difference is that the conch train is a tour while the trolley is more of a hop on and hop off experience. That said, the trolley takes you beyond Old Town thereby showing you more of Key West. If time permits, I highly recommend both options. They both offer 100% money-back guarantees if you're not satisfied. And on a hot day, you will welcome the ride.

Ghosts & Gravestones offers a unique way to chase ghosts and that is on their Trolley of the Doomed. Ride through the streets of Old Town listening to ghost stories. An exclusive tour of one of the most haunted locations on the island, East Martello Fort, is included in this tour. This tour is not recommended for children under the age of 13. www.ghostsandgravestones.com.

Ghost Mysteries Tour is a 90-minute walking tour of Key West's Old Town. www.keywestghostandmysteriestour.com.

Ghost Tours & Hunts is recommended for adults only but ages 16 and up will be allowed. Ghost

hunting equipment is included.
www.keywestghosthunt.com.

Haunted Pub Crawl is an adults-only option for those interested in some "spirited" fun. This 2.5-hour guided tour includes cocktails, contests, a souvenir t-shirt and lots of ghost stories.
www.keywestwalkingtours.com.

Key West Ghost & Mysteries Tour promises "90 minutes of Spirited Tales & Sights" featuring historic Old Town.
www.keywestghostandmysteriestour.com

Old Town Trolley Tours offers another fun way to see Key West. Kids 12 and under ride free and there are senior and military discounts. Like the Conch Train, it lasts 90 minutes if you don't get off. I recommend riding it around the island once and then using it to get around Key West. Passengers are permitted unlimited hop on and hop off privileges at its 13 designated stops. Trolley tickets include admission to the Overseas Railroad Museum. A bonus is a second free day so this may help make up your mind if you'll be staying a few days as it is a free way to get around the island (remember that parking is problematic). Also, the drivers share so much information (both on the conch train and the trolley tours) that it is nearly impossible to absorb it all during one outing. www.trolleytours.com.

The Original Ghost Tours is a 90-minute walking tour that concludes upstairs of the Hard Rock Café. Ghost hunting equipment is included. www.hauntedtours.com.

Highlights:

Hemingway House, Dry Tortugas National Park,
Key West Lighthouse Museum, Key West Butterfly
& Nature Conservancy, Key West Shipwreck
Museum, Key West Tropical Forest & Botanical
Garden, Harry Truman House, Key West Cemetery,
Mel Fisher Maritime Museum, Ripley's Odditorium,
East Martello Museum, Southernmost Point, Sunset
Celebration, ghost tours, Old Town Trolley Tour,
and Conch Train Tour.

www.keywest.com

www.keywestchamber.com

Best Places to Shop and Dine...

Be sure to obtain a comprehensive and up-to-date list of all the restaurants and shops before your visit from www.keywest.com. You can also check out www.keysdining.com.

Best Places for Souvenirs:

*Bahama Village Market (south of Whitehead Street) is the place to go to find souvenir t-shirts, straw hats, beads, crafts, and more.

*Clinton Square Market (Front Street) is an *air-conditioned* mall that offers everything from clothes to sweet treats. Come in and cool off, browse a bit, and enjoy some key lime ice cream.

*Mallory Square (Whitehead Street) has a bit of everything: Conch Store, Sponge Market, Shell Warehouse, Caribbean

Cargo, and much more.
www.mallorysquare.com.

The biggest shopping and dining
forums include the Historic
Waterfront, Simonton Row,
Crowne Plaza La Concha, Truval
Village (art galleries and more),
Searstown Shopping Center,
Overseas Market, and Angela
Street Depot.

**BEST FOOD TRUCK: Garbo's
Grill.** I'm not a big fan of the food
truck craze but I am making an
exception in this case because of their
exceptional food. If you get to Key
West, go to 409 Caroline Street. That
is where the truck is usually parked. If
you don't see it check out their site to
find the new location.
www.garbosgrillkw.com. They serve
lunch and dinner. I recommend their

Yum Yum Shrimp (Korean style) and their Mango Dog. *Yum!*

BEST PLACE TO STAY:
Southernmost House Historic Inn. Dating back to 1896, this inn has hosted five U.S. presidents and once served as a Cuban nightclub. The 18-room inn is located in the heart of Key West so it is within walking distance to many attractions, shops and restaurants and they have a concierge service to assist you with any and all activities and reservations. They offer AAA discounts and some 'Specials' are posted on their website. The best rates are typically offered during the week with the highest rates on weekends. 1400 Duval Street. www.southernmosthouse.com.

BEST CIGARS:
Cigar City has the largest selection of
hand-made cigars on the island. It also
features indoor and outdoor smoking
lounges. Cigar City is open every day
year round. A neat idea for a bachelor
party is their "cigar rollers for all
occasions." 410 Wall Street.
www.cigarcityusa.com.

**BEST SOUVENIR SHOP: 90 Miles
to Cuba.** This is a great shop but the
hours suck. They are open 12 p.m. – 5
p.m. Thursday – Sunday (or whenever
they choose to open and close). What
you'll find if they're open: art &
nautical antiques, handmade modern
& antique jewelry, rare and unusual
books, original & reproduction
graphic art and antique postcards of

Key West & Cuba. 616 Greene Street. http://www.90milestocuba.net/

BEST WATER RESOURCES: For boaters (www.floridakeysboating.com), for fishing (www.fishfloridakeys.com), and for all other water activities (www.floridakeys.noaa.gov).

BEST PLACE TO GET ROWDY: Seriously? You're in Key West so just about anywhere is acceptable but one of the best places is **Sloppy Joe's.** You'll also hear some good music and see lots of Hemingway memorabilia since this was his favorite watering hole. The official beginning of Sloppy Joe's Bar was December 5, 1933–the day Prohibition was repealed. The bar changed locations in 1937 due to a rent increase. Rather than pay it, the proprietor, Joe Russell, moved across the street. By the way, Sloppy Joe's was formerly known as the Blind Pig and Silver Slipper before Hemingway suggested that Joe change the name to Sloppy Joe's. Everyone knows that Papa Hemingway always got what he wanted so the bar became known forevermore as Sloppy Joe's. Whenever I get nostalgia for my time here I just spend some time watching their webcam, https://sloppyjoes.com/web-cams/.

Runner Up: Captain Tony's Saloon at 428 Greene Street was actually the home of the original Sloppy Joe's Bar.

More Popular Nightspots: Hard Rock Café, Fat Tuesday (the place to go for frozen alcoholic drinks), Rick's Key West (is actually eight nightclubs under one roof), Bull & Whistle (three bars in one), Joe's Tap Room (above Sloppy Joe's), and Hog's Breath Saloon (one of my favorites).

If you want to partake in Ernest Hemingway's favorite drink, here's the recipe for Papa Doble:

2-3 jiggers of white Bacardi Rum (depending on how strong you want it)

Juice of ½ grapefruit

Juice of 2 limes

6 drops of maraschino juice

Mix all the ingredients in blender and serve as is to drink like Hemingway or serve over ice.

BEST FRUIT MILKSHAKES: Island Juice Bar Stand in Mallory Square is the perfect remedy for hot, tired tourists. Choose from all kinds of refreshing milkshakes, such as strawberry banana and key lime coconut.

BEST FINE DINING: The Commodore at the marina. This waterfront restaurant is open nightly and offers a great menu, including Sesame-crusted Yellowfin Tuna, Delmonico steak, and 10-ounce Florida Lobster Tail. Cap off your meal with its signature Chocolate Mousse or Key Lime Pie. www.commodorekeywest.com.

BEST SELF-GUIDED TOUR:
Known as Pelican Path, this nifty
brochure shares all the historically
significant structures and streets in
Key West. The self-guided walk
begins and ends at Mallory Square
Steamship Company. The free maps
can be obtained at Mallory Square
Hospitality House or at the Chamber
of Commerce.

BEST VIEW: Now this is a tough
call but overall I think the upper deck
of **Rum Barrel Restaurant & Bar** is
hard to beat. It's at 502 Front Street—
just one block from Duval Street and
Key West Seaport so you are in the
middle of the action and there is live
entertainment nightly. Founded by Pat
Croce and home of the Key West
Gator Club, the Rum Barrel has a
great atmosphere and good food.

BEST FAMILY RESTAURANT:
Two Friends Patio Restaurant is a
family-owned landmark on Front
Street conveniently located between

the seaport and Mallory Square. It is one of the last of the original Old Town Key West restaurants. Dating back to 1967, this charming little restaurant serves breakfast, lunch, and dinner indoors and outdoors. Their prices are not cheap but they are reasonable, especially if you take advantage of their 4-6 p.m. early bird dinner menu. Another perk is their free delivery throughout Key West. www.twofriendskeywest.com.

BEST PLACE FOR AFTER DINNER DRINK: A & B Lobster House has a lovely bar, **Berlin's**, which is the best place to go for dessert wines, cognacs, martinis, and more. A & B was established in 1947 and is still a local favorite. Perks include a great harbor view and being able to smoke a hand-rolled cigar if you like.
www.aandblobsterhouse.com.

Easy Key Lime Pie Recipe

Pie Ingredients:

4 large egg yolks

(1) 14-ounce can of condensed milk

½ cup freshly squeezed key lime juice
(bottled juice can be used but it is better if
you can use fresh key limes)

Beat egg yolks and then add in condensed
milk, blending on low speed. Add lime juice
and make sure well
blended.

To Make the
Crust:

1 cup crushed
graham crackers

3 tbsp. sugar

5 tbsp. melted butter (preferably salted)

Mix all ingredients until well blended. Press
the mixture into a nine-inch pie pan. Bake
pie shell at 350 for ten minutes or until
slightly brown. Let cool before pouring in

pie filling. When ready, add pie filling and bake for ten minutes. Refrigerate pie 4-6 hours before serving. Add real whipped cream and lime slices to garnish. Serve and enjoy!

FYI: Florida Keys Key Lime Pie is more yellow than green so if you want to make sure you're eating the real thing, check the color!

Annual Events

There are hundreds of festivals and special events held year round. Here is a list of some of the biggest and best. See page 244 for more Keys listings and a comprehensive list can be found at www.keywest.com.

Conch Republic Celebration (April) www.conchrepublic.com

World Sailfish Championship (April) www.worldsailfish.com)

Sunset Celebration Welcome the Tall Ships (May) www.sunsetcelebration.com

Cuban American Heritage Festival (May)(www.cubanamericanfestival. com)

Hemingway Days (July) www.fla-keys.com

Ernest Hemingway left Paris in 1928 and came to Key West with his second wife, Pauline. Her family bought Ernest and Pauline a car, paid for an African safari, and a house in the middle of Key West (now the Hemingway House Museum). Life was good. Hemingway spent his mornings writing and his afternoons and evenings hanging with other colorful characters who taught him how to hunt and deep sea fish. These same men joined him most nights at Sloppy Joe's. Although the Papa Doble is said to be his favorite drink it was actually scotch and soda.

The couple typically summered in Wyoming or Europe and wintered in Key West until he divorced Pauline in 1940 and married his third wife, Martha. They moved to Cuba but Pauline stayed in the Key West house until her death in 1951.

In 1964, it was turned into a tourist attraction and has remained one of the most popular island attractions. It is a great tour. Hearing the stories that bring the legendary Hemingway to life, seeing where he lived and worked, and browsing in the gift shop is a must for tourists.

Warning! There are lots of fans but NO air conditioning in the Hemingway House and the tours are always full (of sweaty tourists) so just be forewarned that you will be "a tad warm" during this tour, especially on the second floor.

Key West Food & Wine Festival (Jan)

Key West Lobsterfest (August)

Key West Race Week (Jan) www.premiere-racing.com)

Key West Pridefest (www.pridefestkeywest.com)

FYI: Key West has a large gay population with roughly twenty percent of the residents being gay. www.gaykeywestfl.com

Key West World Championship (November) www.keywestpowerboatraces.com)

Mel Fisher Days (July) (www.melfisher.com)

Key West Brewfest (August)

Fantasy Fest (October)
www.fantasyfest.com

> *FYI: Picture a crazy blend of Carnival, Salem's Halloween Ball, and Mardi Gras and you get the picture.* **Fantasy Fest** *lasts brings in roughly 75,000 tourists. This nine-day countdown to Halloween includes Masked Monday, Fantasy Yacht Race's Victory at Sea, Masked Madness, Pet Masquerade, and concluded with a Royal Coronation Ball during which time a King and Queen of Fantasy Fest are crowned. It's a no holds barred contest that participants take very seriously.*

Key West World Championship Race (Nov) www.superboat.com

Key West Film Festival (Nov)

Pirates in Paradise (Nov/Dec) (www.piratesinparadise.com)

International Sand Art Competition (Dec)

Pirates in Paradise Festival (Dec)
www.piratesinparadise.com

Nutcracker Key West (Dec)
www.keystix.com

New Years Eye Shoe Drop (Dec)
www.keywestcity.com

Florida Keys Seafood Festival (Jan)

Key West Food & Wine Festival (Jan)

Key West Race Week (Jan)

Master Chefs Classic (Jan)

Key West Historic House & Garden Tours (Jan) www.oirf.org

Civil War Heritage Days (Feb)
www.forttaylor.org

Tennessee Williams Birthday Celebration (March)

FYI: Key West has more than 2,500 historic buildings, such as Harry Truman's Little White House Museum, Audubon House, Southernmost House, and Hemingway House.

While there are a few theaters scattered throughout the Keys, most are located in Key West:

Key West Fringe Theater hosts fringe performances (think non-traditional theater in non-theater settings throughout Key West). www.fringetheater.org.

Key West Theater shows original play and musicals, as well as old movies, concerts and special shows. 512 Eaton Street. www.thekeywesttheater.com/

Red Barn Theatre is small but puts on big shows. 319 Duvall Street. www.redbarntheatre.com/

Tennessee Williams Theatre hosts many visiting theater troupes. The theater has been around since 1980 when the Tennessee Williams play "Will Mr. Merriweather Return from Memphis?" debuted. 5901 College Road.
www.tennesseewilliamstheatre.com/

The Studios of Key West offers a bit of everything from circus arts to burlesque. 533 Eaton Street.
http://tskw.org/

Waterfront Playhouse is renowned thanks to the Key West Players, who are the oldest continually operating theater company in Florida. The 150-seat theater often sells out thanks to the performers and the theater's location, which is adjacent to Mallory Square. 310 Wall Street.
www.waterfrontplayhouse.org.

TERRANCE ZEPKE

JUST FOR FUN...

Florida Keys Wildlife Checklist

Author's Note: This list is not meant to be comprehensive but rather a fun checklist of the more commonly seen species.

____**Atlantic spotted dolphin**
____**Atlantic bottlenose dolphin**

____**West Indian Manatee**

____**Key Deer**

____**Wild Turkey**

____**American Alligator**

____**Sea Turtle**

____**Hawksbill Sea Turtle**

____**Leatherback Sea Turtle**

____**Atlantic Ridley Sea Turtle**

_____Loggerhead Sea Turtle

_____Green Iguana

_____Gopher Tortoise

_____Florida Box Turtle

_____Florida Red Belly Turtle

_____Eastern Indigo Snake

_____Atlantic Saltmarsh Snake

_____Southern Bald Eagle

_____Peregrine Falcon

_____Roseate Tern

_____Brown Pelican

_____Florida Sandhill Crane

_____Green Heron

_____Great Blue Heron

____**Little Blue Heron**

____**Night Heron**

____**Lower Keys Marsh Rabbit**

____**Barbados Yellow Warbler**

____**Giant Swallowtail Butterfly**

____**Zebra Longwing (state butterfly)**

____**Zebra Swallowtail Butterfly**

____**Queen Butterfly**

____**Great Southern White Butterfly**

____**White Peacock Butterfly**

____**American Crocodile (seen much less commonly than American Alligator)**

_____ **Florida Panther**

_____**Glossy Ibis**

_____**Snowy Egret**

_____**Great Egret**

_____**Cattle Egret**

_____**Red-bellied Woodpecker**

_____**Key Largo Cotton Mouse**

> *FYI: Roughly 70 species of animals found in the Everglades and Florida Keys are endangered. Some species you hope not to see include fire ants, cicadas, no-see-ums (biting gnats), mosquitoes, Key Largo Woodrat, Florida Cottonmouth (venomous snake), Pygmy Rattler (venomous snake), wild hogs, and chiggers.*

*   *   *

How to Talk Like a Local...

I try to learn some phrases and common words wherever I travel. If traveling where English is spoken, I still try to learn the "local lingo." Here is a list of common terms that will have you speaking like a local:

Alligator Alley (Everglades Parkway): Nickname for part of I-75 that extends from Naples through the Everglades to Fort Lauderdale.

Airboat (Swamp Boat): Open boat with giant caged, rear-mounted propeller that allows it to go fast and navigate shallow water and marshes.

Backcountry: islet waters of Florida Bay

Bayside: anything on the opposite side (coast) of Atlantic Ocean (which is Oceanside), which would be Florida Bay in the Upper Keys and Gulf of Mexico in the Middle and Lower Keys

Bone Cay: This is a nickname for Key West.

Coconut telegraph: local gossip (word of mouth)

Conch (pronounced "konk"): person born on Key West who thinks differently from many, especially conservatives. The term dates back to mid-1600s when British colonists declared themselves tax exempt and free to worship as they pleased.

Conch: In addition to meaning a native Key Wester, the term also refers to a gastropod that is indigenous to the Keys and Caribbean.

FYI: Florida Keys Queen Conch is seldom harvested due to its rarity. Most conch served in the Keys is imported from the Caribbean.

Conch Republic: The Florida Keys attempted permanent secession from the U.S. in 1982. During this brief time, the micronation called itself the Conch Republic.

Conch Wannabees: People who want to live in Key West and plan to do so one day.

Freshwater Conchs: People who have migrated to Key West after visiting and never wanting to leave.

Floribbean cuisine: The Keys have a cuisine that is a blend of fresh Florida seafood and produce with American, Caribbean, European, and Latin American influences.

Florida lobster (Spiny Lobster): What makes this different from "true" lobsters is that these crustaceans lack claws and have long, thick, spiny antennae, hence the name.

Hammock: hardwood tropical forest

Key: low-lying island composed mostly of sand or coral. The name is derived from Spanish word "cayo," meaning little island.

Keys Disease: Life is different on the Keys and overindulgence and having *too* good a time can become a problem. You know you are suffering from Keys Disease if you spend most nights doing the Duval Crawl (frequenting Duval Street night spots).

MM: MM stands for "mile marker." This is how locations are designated in the Keys. Travelers follow the green signs that will have decreasing numbers as you journey down U.S. 1 until you will see MM0 at the Key West waterfront.

Manatee (Sea Cow): The Manatee is the state mammal and is also endangered.

Participants often see these during eco-tours of the Everglades.

Mangrove Swamp: These swamps are home to odd-looking black, red, and white mangrove trees.

No-see-um: tiny biting gnat that is prevalent in the Florida Keys

Old Key West: Natives refer to Old Town as Old Key West.

Overseas Highway (U.S. 1): This is the popular term assigned to U.S. 1, which extends from Key Largo to Key West.

Seven Mile Bridge: This bridge connects the Middle Keys to the Lower Keys at Marathon. It is part of the Overseas Highway. As you come down U.S. 1 you will see a bridge off to the right, which is the old Seven Mile Bridge. It is only open to fishermen, joggers, walkers, and cyclists.

FYI: If you're planning on visiting in April be aware that the Seven Mile Bridge Run is held annually and the bridge is closed for much of that day.

Ship Ashore!: The Keys originated as wrecking communities. Ships often sank in this area. When this happened, locals cried out *"Ship Ashore!"* and sprang into action. Boats and crews were dispensed to salvage whatever they could. This was a profitable enterprise for a long time.

Southernmost Point: A huge, concrete buoy signifies the southernmost point of the

U.S. which is at the junction of Key West's South and Whitehead Streets and just ninety miles from Cuba.

The Rock: Another word for The Keys.

The Stretch: The area of highway that goes into and out of the Keys so roughly MM 123 (Florida City) to MM 105 Key Largo.

*　　*　　*

Florida Keys Quiz

1. Which famed Hollywood boat can be found in Key Largo?
   a. *USS Arizona*
   b. *Love Boat*
   c. *African Queen*
   d. *Titanic*

2. John D. Pennekamp State Park is named after John D. Pennekamp. What was his profession?
   a. Newspaper editor
   b. Biologist
   c. Realtor
   d. Mayor

3. Islamodora is known for what?
   a. Sport fishing Capital
   b. Diving Capital
   c. Conch Capital
   d. Bird watching Capital

4. The Keys are home to an ecosystem that has dense trees and low elevation. What are these ecosystems called?
   a. Glades
   b. Isles
   c. Hardwood hammocks
   d. Mango groves

5. What was the population of the Key Deer before the establishment of the Key Deer Refuge?
   a. More than 1,000
   b. More than 500
   c. More than 100
   d. More than 25

6. Henry Flagler established the Overseas Railroad using some of his vast fortune. How did he make so much money?
   a. railroad
   b. oil
   c. newspapers
   d. salt production

7. What is the first key you come to?
   a. Key West
   b. Key Largo
   c. Pigeon Key
   d. Deer Key

8. How far is Key West from the Equator?
   a. 337 miles
   b. 512 miles
   c. 1,699 miles
   d. 3,298 miles

9. What is the closest key to the Dry Tortugas National Park?
   a. Marathon
   b. Key West
   c. Islamorada
   d. Key Largo

10. Besides his writing, what else is Hemingway's legacy?
    a. Six-toed cats
    b. Lighthouse museum
    c. Giant statue in Old Town
    d. Exotic bird sanctuary

Bonus question: Can you name one of Ernest Hemingway's book titles?

Bonus question: Can you name a threatened or endangered Keys species?

Florida Keys Quiz Answers

1. c
2. a
3. a
4. c
5. d
6. b
7. b
8. c
9. b
10. a

*   *   *

Important Information:

What to Pack...

- Bug Spray with DEET, picaridin, or oil of lemon eucalyptus as an active ingredient
- 30 or 50 SPF Sunscreen lotion
- Wide-brimmed Hat or visor
- Long sleeve shirt
- Long Pants
- Sunglasses
- Shoes for the beach (some beaches are rocky)
- Good walking/hiking socks & shoes or boots
- Flip flops or sandals

- Camera and accessories
- Bottled water
- Rain gear
- An awning for shade and/or rain (camping)
- Extra dry clothing in a dry bag
- First aid kit
- Bathing suit
- T-shirts and shorts
- Dressy casual outfit if planning on fine dining
- Pajamas
- Toiletries
- Medications
- Books, magazines or tablet/reader
- Cell phone
- Cash/credit cards
- Travel documents
- Undergarments
- Chargers and extra batteries
- After bite stick

If you're planning on doing any special interest activities, be sure to pack what you need for that, such as a prescription mask if going snorkeling or shark diving. All companies provide wetsuits and masks but not prescription masks.

*converters and adaptors if you are visiting from overseas and have an electric razor, curling iron, mobile phone/tablet, hair dryer or if you think you'll need to charge your phone, camera batteries, or will have some type of medical equipment that requires an outlet.

TERRANCE TALKS TRAVEL: A POCKET GUIDE TO THE FLORIDA KEYS

FYI: Be sure to check for the latest updates from TSA so that you know what you can and can't take on the plane in your carry-on bag or pack in your suitcase. You don't want your sunscreen or bug spray confiscated! Also, you should check with your airline regarding their latest baggage restrictions (and baggage fees). There is a weight limit and acceptable sizes for both carry-on bags and checked luggage, which varies according to the airline. Certain items are banned or restricted to three ounces or less and limited to certain types of containers, as determined by TSA. These restrictions are subject to change periodically.
http://www.tsa.gov/traveler-information/packing-tip

* * *

TRAVEL DOCUMENTS: Be sure to keep a copy of your itinerary and emergency contact information with you at all times. Keep copies of every ticket and confirmation to show if needed. You must have a valid passport to enter the U.S. For more on passports and visas, http://www.passportsandvisas.com/ Give a copy of your itinerary to a relative or close friend.

FYI: Don't forget you can buy a souvenir Conch Republic passport!

TRAVEL INSURANCE: Anytime you travel, you may want to consider buying travel insurance. Do a little research or ask your travel agent for recommendations. www.Travelexinsurance.com and www.travelinsured.com are two good options.

TRAVEL WARNINGS: At the time of publication, there were no local mosquito-borne Zika virus disease cases reported in US states, but there have been travel-associated cases. For the latest check http://www.cdc.gov/zika/. Before any travel it is advisable to check with www.cdv.gov and http://travel.state.gov.

VACCINATIONS: None are necessary at this time but you can check with http://www.vaccines.gov/travel/ and http://wwwnc.cdc.gov/travel to verify the latest requirements.

FOOD & WATER: There are currently no warnings for food or water in the Keys.

THE PEOPLE: It goes without saying—yet I am saying it because it is such an important point—travelers should always be respectful of other cultures and of other travelers. Your behavior reflects on all people of your native country. Not only should your behavior be exemplary, but you should also dress appropriately. In Key West, this is not a problem since it is casual so sleeveless tops and shorts are acceptable most places. Be advised that Key West is a melting pot of different cultures and ideologies. Don't go if you're going to have a problem with that or if you can't obey rules. We were on a conch train (with a clearly marked "No Cellphones" sign and a woman in front of us got on the phone and talked for at least thirty minutes of the tour. Talk about disruptive to the rest of us! Since she was sitting in front of the sign I'm pretty sure she saw it but chose to disregard it. Please don't be "that person."

SAFETY: As with any travel, you are putting yourself out there. Despite any attempts you make, it will probably be obvious that you are a tourist so be sure to exercise common sense. Crime can happen in even the safest places, so pay attention. Don't wander off down a dark, side street alone. If you're out and about and notice that you have entered a desolate or seedy-looking area, hightail it back to a congested area. Don't count your money on the street corner. Don't wear expensive jewelry. Don't call attention to yourself. Don't carry a lot money in your pocket or bag. Be careful to safeguard your passport and other travel documents.

ATTITUDE: Traveling can be so rewarding and fun. But at times, it can be challenging, like when a flight is delayed or canceled. Or if you get stuck in traffic. Or the air conditioning is not working in your room. Or if you experience other problems. Most are just "hiccups" and can be overcome fairly easy. You have to be flexible and adaptable when traveling to the other side of the world.

Think of all the great stories you can tell when you get home. Sometimes, what seems like a bad situation can lead to something good. I've met some of the best people and had some of the exceptional experiences as a result of a detour or delay.

HEALTH: If you have a health condition, such as heart trouble or diabetes, you should consult your doctor before taking any trip or tackling any adventurous activities. You also need to check with the authorities to find out if you need a letter from your doctor (if taking injections or narcotics) and there are airline rules about carrying oxygen and some types of inhalers. It is best not to start new medications before traveling in case of adverse reactions.

MONEY: Make sure you have enough in the right denomination. I recommend the 1/3 system, which is 1/3 cash in small bills and 1/3 credit card (two different ones) and 1/3 travelers cheques. This is for international travelers. If traveling within your own country, you can stick to half cash and half credit cards. I like to do this because you may need cash somewhere that credit is not accepted or your card could get rejected, so it is best to have some cash on hand.

You need to authorize your credit card company to approve travel transactions as most will block them now due to credit card fraud. You don't have to be overseas or even have high usage for the algorithms to sense "suspicious activity." Even if you have notified your card company they may 'freeze' your account.

That's why I recommend a back-up credit card. Check the transaction fees and rates (and balances and rewards) before deciding which card to take.

You can even opt for a pre-paid travel credit card. Both Visa and MasterCard are widely accepted, but Discover and American Express are not as widely accepted.

You can exchange cash at exchange bureaus at the airport or at a bank or even your hotel. Make sure you do that before you leave for a less populated or remote destination on your trip.

Keep your contact information separate from your traveler's cheques and credit cards. If they get stolen, you will have the information you need to replace the traveler's cheques and cancel the credit cards. You don't want to wait until you get home to do that as it will be too late by that time.

Sample 7-Day Itinerary

This itinerary can be altered to suit your interests, timeline, and budget. Build onto this sample itinerary if you are able to stay longer than one week. The Florida Keys are a long journey for most of us so I don't recommend going for less than a week. Scale back on optional activities if you're looking to save money. Choose more economical digs rather than pricey resorts if your budget is limited. There are so many wonderful things to see and do in the Keys (and so many ways to experience them) that you can't go wrong unless you don't stay long enough or don't do sufficient planning.

Day #1: Arrive a.m. in Fort Lauderdale. If flying into Miami or driving to Florida, be sure to spend the night in Fort Lauderdale so that you can make the scenic drive during daylight hours or so that you can do a safari while in the Everglades area.

Day #2: Depart early for full day eco-safari in Everglades. Overnight in Jules Undersea Lodge at Key Largo, which is thirty miles from Homestead.

Day #3: Go snorkeling or diving at John Pennekamp Coral Reef State Park and/or take a glass-bottomed boat ride. Spend the night in a resort in Islamorada or Marathon where you'll have sundowner drinks and nice dinner.

Day #4: Drive down Lower Keys, stopping at Deer Key Wildlife

Refuge. Arrive in Key West in time for a night ghost tour.

Day #5: Hit the ground running! As you can see from my Key West chapter, you will have to be selective as there is no way you can do it all. So make a list of what you want to see and do and then do as much as time permits.

Day #6: Spend another day hitting the highlights of Key West.

Day #7: Spend the morning enjoying Key West and then start drive back up the Keys, spending the night in Fort Lauderdale or Miami, or if driving all the way home, spend the night anywhere on the way.

If you have an additional day or two you can take that time to visit the Dry Tortugas or squeeze in some more sights and shopping. Or you can take that time to explore another part of the

Keys on your way home, such as Deer Key Refuge or Islamorada.

FYI: You may want to do some research as to what is on your route home in case you'd like to make a quick sightseeing stop or plan a layover. It is...

27 miles from Miami to Ft. Lauderdale

30 miles from Everglades (Homestead) to Key Largo)

58 miles from Miami to Key Largo

100 miles from Key Largo to Key West

160 miles from Miami to Key West

*   *   *

Resources

There are many good resources and references about the Florida Keys and its history. Here are a few recommendations:

Weather (Florida Keys)
http://www.go-florida.com/Key-West/Weather/

Sunset Celebration (Key West)
https://www.mallorysquare.com/sunset-celebration/

Art Galleries (Key West)
https://www.mallorysquare.com/key-west-art-galleries/

Florida Keys Webcams
http://www.fla-keys.com/webcams/

Florida Keys Maps
http://www.fla-keys.com/maps/

Florida Keys Tourism Council
www.fla-keys.com

Miami & Area Beaches
https://www.mallorysquare.com/key-west-art-galleries/

Google Maps, www.maps.google.com

*   *   *

Here is a list of good publications:

MAPS

Free interactive maps of Florida Keys can be found at http://www.floridakeys.com/floridakeysmaps.htm

REFERENCES

Free Fort Lauderdale Planning Guide, http://www.sunny.org/free-visitor-guide/

Fodor's Miami Travel Guide, http://www.fodors.com/world/north-america/usa/florida/miami

FUN FLORIDA KEYS BOOKS

Last Train to Paradise: Henry Flagler and the Spectacular Rise and Fall of the Railroad That Crossed an Ocean (Les Standiford)

Hemingway's Key West (Stuart B. McIver)

It Happened in the Florida Keys (David L. Sloan)

Crazy in Paradise (Deborah Brown)

Bad Monkey (Carl Hiaasen)

Turtle in Paradise (Jennifer L. Holm)

*   *   *

Special Dates & Events

The following is a list of public holidays that most museums, parks and government offices observe:

New Year's Day (January 1)

Christmas Day (December 25)

Thanksgiving (4th Thursday in November)

*   *   *

This is a list of major annual events throughout the Keys (more special events can be found on page 196):

Mel Fisher Maritime Museum Free Lecture Series (Year-round)

Civil War Heritage Days Festival
(February)

Annual Key West House & Garden Tour (February)

Happy Birthday Tennessee Williams (March)

Annual Florida Keys Ocean Festival & Waterfront Craft Show (April)

Naval Air Station Key West Southernmost Air Spectacular (April)

Annual Conch Republic Independence Celebration (April)

Key West Pride (June)

Annual Mystery Writers' Key West Fest (June)

Key West Africana Festival (June)

Fourth Annual Key Lime Festival (July)

Hemingway Days (July)

Bacardi Oakheart Key West Marlin Tournament (July)

Annual Key West Fantasy Fest (October)

Annual Key West World Championship Races – Super Boat International (November)

Key West Triathlon and Expo (December)

For a complete list visit http://www.fla-keys.com/calendarofevents/

*   *   *

A Picture Is Worth

A Thousand Words...

Aaahhhhhhhhh!

Dolphin Research Center (Marathon)

Dry Tortugas National Park

Hemingway House

Bahia Honda State Park (Big Pine Key)

Christ Statue of the Abyss

(Key Largo)

Alligator Reef Lighthouse

(Islamorada)

Key Deer (Lower Florida Keys)

Sportfishing on Islamorada

**Airboat rides are thrilling and the best
way to get up close to wildlife in
Everglades National Park.**

Aerial view of Key West

Southernmost Hotel (Key West)

**The Overseas Highway (US 1) connects
the Keys to one another and to the
mainland.**

A great sightseeing option in Key West is the Conch Train Tour. Pictured in the background is the iconic Sloppy Joe's Bar.

**West Indian Manatees are one of many
species of wildlife you may see while in
the Florida Keys.**

TERRANCE ZEPKE

There is a 99% chance you will see a gator while in the Keys.

**Sunset Celebration is held nightly in
Mallory Square, Key West.**

**A "must do" in Key West is to pose beside
the SOUTHERNMOST POINT.**

**One of the best diving areas in America is
John Pennekamp Coral Reef State Park.
(Key Largo)**

There are eight buildings on five-acre Pigeon Key that are on the National Register of Historic Places.

**The Keys has been voted the #1 fishing
spot in America.**

**Fort Jefferson is part of the Dry Tortugas
National Park, which can be reached by
ferry from Key West.**

There are hundreds of special events and festivals held throughout the Keys, such as the International Sand Castle Competition.

This is not a replica. This is the original, restored boat from the 1951 film, African Queen, starring Humphrey Bogart and Katherine Hepburn. The boat can be rented out for special occasions.

African Queen

On route to the Keys you should visit the Coral Castle in Miami. It was built by one man using only manmade tools.

Dead end!

US 1 (Overseas Highway) ends in Key West.

**A great way to learn about local legends
and folklore is to take a ghost walk/tour,
such as the Ghosts & Gravestones trolley
tour.**

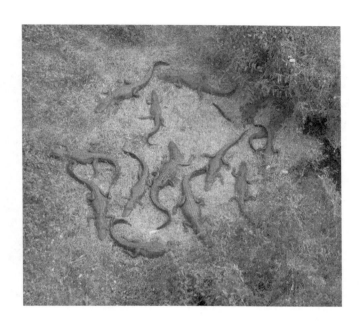

I did mention that there's a 99% chance you'll see at least one gator while in the Everglades, didn't I?

The elusive Florida Panther

Key West Lighthouse Museum

**There is no shortage of cold, tropical
drinks to cool you down in Key West.**

TERRANCE ZEPKE

*All maps and photos are courtesy of The
Florida Keys Tourism Newsroom and
Wikipedia unless otherwise noted.

Dear Reader,

Thank you for buying or borrowing **Terrance Talks Travel: A Pocket Guide to the Florida Keys.** Isn't it an incredible place? There is just so much to see and do! I hope you get a chance to visit and discover it for yourself.

I spent a great deal of time compiling this information into what I believe is an easy-to-read, useful reference. I would love to hear from you if you'd like to post a question or comment about this book or anything travel-related on www.terrancetalkstravel.com. I do respond to all comments. If you'd like to learn more about travel be sure to sign up for my *Terrance Talks Travel* blog, which will also alert you when the latest episodes of my travel show are available. As a bonus, you will receive a FREE 50-page Travel Report when you sign up!

I would also like to ask you to please share your feedback about this book on Amazon or your favorite bookseller so that other readers might discover this title too.

Authors appreciate readers more than you realize and we dearly love and depend upon good reviews! If you've never posted a review before it is easy to do...just tell folks what you liked or didn't like about this book and why you (hopefully) recommend it.
http://www.amazon.com/Terrance-Zepke/e/B000APJNIA/ref=sr_ntt_srch_lnk_3?qid=1438800300&sr=8-3

Thank you again for your interest and here's hoping you experience many remarkable journeys...

Terrance

Series Reading Order

& Guide

TERRANCE ZEPKE

Series List

Most Haunted Series

Terrance Talks Travel Series

Spookiest Series

Stop Talking Series

Carolinas for Kids Series

Ghosts of the Carolinas Series

Books & Guides in the Carolinas Series

& More Books!

≈

Introduction

Here is a list of titles by Terrance Zepke. They are presented in chronological order although they do not need to be read in any particular order.

Also included is an author bio and some other information you may find helpful.

All books are available as ebooks and print books. They can be found on Amazon, Barnes and Noble, Kobo, Apple iBooks, Smashwords, or through your favorite bookseller.

Visit her Author Page at
http://www.amazon.com/Terrance-
Zepke/e/B000APJNIA/.

You can also connect with
Terrance on Twitter
@terrancezepke or on

www.facebook.com/terrancezepke

www.pinterest.com/terrancezepke

www.goodreads.com/terrancezepke

Sign up for weekly email notifications of the **Terrance Talks Travel** blog to be the first to learn about new episodes of her travel show, get hundreds of cheap travel tips and FREE REPORTS, and discover her TRIP PICK OF THE WEEK at www.terrancetalkstravel.com or sign up for her **Mostly Ghostly** blog at www.terrancezepke.com.

≈

You can follow her travel show,
TERRANCE TALKS TRAVEL:
ÜBER ADVENTURES on
www.blogtalkradio.com/terrancetalkstravel
or subscribe to it at **iTunes.**

Terrance Zepke is co-host of the writing show, **A WRITER'S JOURNEY: FROM BLANK PAGE TO PUBLISHED,** at **iTunes** or on www.terrancezepke.com.

AUTHOR BIO

Terrance Zepke studied Journalism at the University of Tennessee and later received a Master's degree in Mass Communications from the University of South Carolina. She studied parapsychology at the renowned Rhine Research Center.

Zepke spends much of her time happily traveling around the world but always returns home to the Carolinas where she lives part-time in both states. She has written hundreds of articles and close to three dozen books. She is the host of *Terrance Talks Travel: Über Adventures* and co-host of *A Writer's Journey: From Blank Page to Published*. Additionally, this award-winning and best-selling author has been featured in many publications and programs, such as NPR, CNN, The Washington Post, Associated Press, Travel with Rick

Steves, Around the World, Publishers Weekly, World Travel & Dining with Pierre Wolfe, Good Morning Show, The Learning Channel, and The Travel Channel.

When she's not investigating haunted places, searching for pirate treasure, or climbing lighthouses, she is most likely packing for her next adventure to some far flung place, such as Reyjavik or Kwazulu Natal. Some of her favorite adventures include piranha fishing on the Amazon, shark cage diving in South Africa, hiking the Andes Mountains Inca Trail, camping in the Himalayas, and dog-sledding in the Arctic Circle.

According to Zepke, her favorite haunted place is the Stanley Hotel and the creepiest overnight ghost investigation she ever did was the Trans-Allegheny Lunatic Asylum. Her favorite island in the U.S. is Kiawah (SC) and outside of the U.S. it is Madagascar (Africa), favorite city in the U.S. is Charleston (SC) and her favorite international city is London, and her favorite adventure destination is Africa, especially southern and East Africa. While she will rough it for a good adventure, Zepke does enjoy five-star cruises, first class, and champagne too.

≈

MOST HAUNTED SERIES

A Ghost Hunter's Guide to the Most Haunted Places in America (2012)
https://read.amazon.com/kp/embed?asin=B0085SG22O&preview=newtab&linkCode=kpe&ref_=cm_sw_r_kb_d p_zerQwb1AMJoR4

A Ghost Hunter's Guide to the Most Haunted Houses in America (2013)
https://read.amazon.com/kp/embed?asin=B00C3PUMGC&preview=newtab&linkCode=kpe&ref_=cm_sw_r_kb_d p_BfrQwb1WF1Y6T

A Ghost Hunter's Guide to the Most Haunted Hotels & Inns in America (2014)
https://read.amazon.com/kp/embed?asin=B00C3PUMGC&preview=newtab&linkCode=kpe

≈

TERRANCE TALKS TRAVEL SERIES

Terrance Talks Travel: A Pocket Guide to South Africa (2015)
https://read.amazon.com/kp/embed?asin=B00PSTFTLI&preview=newtab&linkCode=kpe&ref_=cm_sw_r_kb_dp_pirQwb12XZX65

Terrance Talks Travel: A Pocket Guide to African Safaris (2015)
https://read.amazon.com/kp/embed?asin=B00PSTFZSA&preview=newtab&linkCode=kpe&ref_=cm_sw_r_kb_dp_jhrQwb0P8Z87G

Terrance Talks Travel: A Pocket Guide to Adventure Travel (2015)
https://read.amazon.com/kp/embed?asin=B00UKMAVQG&preview=newtab&linkCode=kpe&ref_=cm_sw_r_kb_dp_ThrQwb1PVVZAZ

Terrance Talks Travel: A Pocket Guide to Florida Keys (including Key West & Everglades) (2016)

http://www.amazon.com/Terrance-Talks-Travel-Including-Everglades-ebook/dp/B01EWHML58/ref=sr_1_1?s=books&ie=UTF8&qid=1461897775&sr=1-1&keywords=terrance+talks+travel%3A+a+pocket+guide+to+the+florida+keys

SPOOKIEST SERIES

Spookiest Lighthouses (2013)
https://read.amazon.com/kp/embed?
asin=B00EAAQA2S&preview

Spookiest Battlefields (2015)
https://read.amazon.com/kp/embed?
asin=B00XUSWS3G&preview=newtab
&linkCode=kpe&ref_=cm_sw_r_kb_d
p_okrQwb0TR9F8M

Spookiest Cemeteries (2016)

https://read.amazon.com/kp/embed?
asin=B01D0FP498&preview=newtab&
linkCode=kpe&ref_=cm_sw_r_kb_dp_
u.9ixb09KXSSQ

≈

STOP TALKING SERIES

Stop Talking & Start Writing Your Book (2015)
https://read.amazon.com/kp/embed?asin=B012YHTIAY&preview=newtab&linkCode=kpe&ref_=cm_sw_r_kb_dp_qlrQwb1N7G3YF

Stop Talking & Start Publishing Your Book (2015)
https://read.amazon.com/kp/embed?asin=B013HHV1LE&preview=newtab&linkCode=kpe&ref_=cm_sw_r_kb_dp_WlrQwb1F63MFD

Stop Talking & Start Selling Your Book (2015)
https://read.amazon.com/kp/embed?asin=B015YAO33K&preview=newtab&linkCode=kpe&ref_=cm_sw_r_kb_dp_ZkrQwb188J8BE

≈

CAROLINAS FOR KIDS SERIES

Lighthouses of the Carolinas for Kids
(2009)
http://www.amazon.com/Lighthouse
s-Carolinas-Kids-Terrance-
Zepke/dp/1561644293/ref=asap_bc?i
e=UTF8

Pirates of the Carolinas for Kids
(2009)
https://read.amazon.com/kp/embed?
asin=B01BJ3VSWK&preview=newtab
&linkCode=kpe&ref_=cm_sw_r_kb_d
p_rGrXwboXDTSTA

Ghosts of the Carolinas for Kids (2011)
https://read.amazon.com/kp/embed?
asin=B01BJ3VSVQ&preview=newtab&
linkCode=kpe&ref_=cm_sw_r_kb_dp_
XLrXwboE7N1AK

≈

GHOSTS OF THE CAROLINAS SERIES

Ghosts of the Carolina Coasts (1999)
http://www.amazon.com/Ghosts-Carolina-Coasts-Terrance-Zepke/dp/1561641758/ref=asap_bc?ie=UTF8

The Best Ghost Tales of South Carolina (2004)
http://www.amazon.com/Best-Ghost-Tales-South-Carolina/dp/1561643068/ref=asap_bc?ie=UTF8

Ghosts & Legends of the Carolina Coasts (2005)
https://read.amazon.com/kp/embed?asin=B01AGQJABW&preview=newtab&linkCode=kpe&ref_=cm_sw_r_kb_dp_VKrXwb1Q09794

TERRANCE ZEPKE

The Best Ghost Tales of North Carolina
(2006)

https://read.amazon.com/kp/embed?
asin=B01BJ3VSV6&preview=newtab&l
inkCode=kpe&ref_=cm_sw_r_kb_dp_
6IrXwboXKT90Q

≈

BOOKS & GUIDES FOR THE CAROLINAS SERIES

Pirates of the Carolinas (2005)
http://www.amazon.com/Pirates-Carolinas-Terrance-Zepke/dp/1561643440/ref=asap_bc?ie=UTF8

Coastal South Carolina: Welcome to the Lowcountry (2006)
http://www.amazon.com/Coastal-South-Carolina-Welcome-Lowcountry/dp/1561643483/ref=asap_bc?ie=UTF8

Coastal North Carolina: Its Enchanting Islands, Towns & Communities (2011)
http://www.amazon.com/Coastal-North-Carolina-Terrance-Zepke/dp/1561645117/ref=asap_bc?ie=UTF8

TERRANCE ZEPKE

Lighthouses of the Carolinas: A Short History & Guide (2011)

https://read.amazon.com/kp/embed?as
in=B01AGQJA7G&preview=newtab
&linkCode=kpe&ref_=cm_sw_r_kb_
dp_UHrXwb09A22P1

≈

MORE BOOKS BY TERRANCE ZEPKE

*Fiction books written under a pseudonym

Lowcountry Voodoo: Tales, Spells & Boo Hags (2009)
https://read.amazon.com/kp/embed? asin=B018WAGUC6&preview=newtab &linkCode=kpe&ref_=cm_sw_r_kb_d p_UmrQwb19AVSYG

The Encyclopedia of Cheap Travel: Save Up to 90% on Lodging, Flights, Tours, Cruises & More! (2011)
https://read.amazon.com/kp/embed? asin=B005WKGNKY&preview=newta b&linkCode=kpe&ref_=cm_sw_r_kb_ dp_InrQwb18QTWGS

TERRANCE ZEPKE

Ghosts of Savannah (2012)
http://www.amazon.com/Ghosts-Savannah-Terrance-Zepke/dp/1561645303/ref=asap_bc?ie=UTF8

Message from the Author

Since I have written so many books I often get asked for writing advice. My answer is simple. Write about what you are passionate about. Don't try to cash in on the latest trend or most lucrative genre. Stick to what you know and love. This will shine through in your writing, which will help you connect with your audience.

If you're like me and you have a lot of interests, then by all means feel free to write in more than one genre. If you are considering pursuing writing in trans-genre be aware that you will have to work a lot harder to appeal to different audiences. I have to maintain two different websites and write two blogs due to my diverse audience. On www.terrancezepke.com I feature my paranormal book series,

Ghost Town, Halloween Help and
my *Mostly Ghostly* blog. On
www.terrancetalkstravel.com the
content relates to my travel titles, my
Terrance Talks Travel blog, travel
reports, and **Über Adventures Show**.

This brings me to another popular
question. What is my favorite book?
This is going to sound like a cop out
but they all are near and dear to me.
Seriously! My publisher does not
assign me book projects. I choose my
own projects, so it is something I am
knowledgeable and passionate about
or I wouldn't have chosen to tackle it.
I really enjoy researching and writing
the ghost books. What's not to like? I
get to poke around in creepy
cemeteries, spooky lighthouses, old
asylums, and haunted houses
searching for restless spirits—and on
occasion I have found them too! I get
to research the history of these places

and being a huge history buff that is exciting as the investigations.

I am passionate about all my travel books. I love sharing my passion for travel and of specific destinations and types of travel. I am so proud and excited about my **Terrance Talks Travel** book series. The first book, *Terrance Talks Travel: A Pocket Guide to South Africa*, soon became an Amazon #1 bestseller and it remains one of my best-selling books. That is exciting for me as it shows me that I have adequately conveyed my love and knowledge of South Africa to my readers.

But every book holds a special place in my heart. *Lighthouses of the Carolinas* was the first book I ever wrote so that makes is near and dear to me, especially since the second edition came out recently. *Ghosts of the Carolina Coasts* is the first ghost book I ever wrote and remains my best-selling ghost book even after all these years, so I will always have a special fondness for it. Plus, I'm a Carolina girl so I'm into researching, visiting, writing and talking about the Carolinas, especially the coastal area.

If you're like to know more about me or any of these titles, you can check out www.terrancezepke.com or www.terrancetalkstravel.com. You can also find lengthy descriptions and "look inside" options through most online booksellers. Please note that links to book previews have been included for your convenience.

I hope this guide introduces you to some titles you didn't even know about or at the very least lets you know about more ways you can connect with me. Authors love to hear from readers. We truly appreciate you more than you'll ever know. Please feel free to send me a comment or question via the comment form found on every page on my websites or follow me on your favorite social media. Don't forget that you can also listen to my writing podcast, **A Writer's Journey**, on iTunes, or my travel show, **Terrance Talks Travel: Über Adventures** on Blog Talk Radio. The best way to make sure you don't miss any episodes of these shows, new book releases and giveaways, contests, my TRIP PICK OF THE WEEK, cheap travel tips, free travel reports, my annual Countdown to Halloween, and much more is to subscribe to ***Terrance Talks Travel*** on www.terrancetalkstravel.com or ***A Writer's Journey***, and/or ***Mostly***

Ghostly on <u>www.terrancezepke.com</u>.

Thanks for your interest and Happy Reading!

Terrance

Sneak Peak

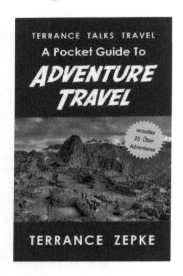

The following is an excerpt from
***Terrance Talks Travel: A Pocket
Guide To Adventure Travel*** which
shares everything you need to know
about adventure travel, including what
it is, how to plan and pack for it, and a
list of the 'Top Twenty-Five' U.S.
and worldwide adventures.

TERRANCE ZEPKE

#4: THE AZORES

Angra do Heroísmo is the oldest town in the archipelago of the Azores

Why: Ancient people believed these islands denoted the end of the world. Mythologists swear they are the remains of the lost continent of Atlantis. It has been dubbed "Europe's last great island adventure."

Located 1,000 miles west of Portugal in the Atlantic Ocean, lies an unspoiled archipelago known as The Azores. This Mediterranean oasis is comprised of nine unique islands filled with volcanos, hot mineral springs, geysers, crystal blue lakes, quaint sea towns, waterfalls, caves, walking trails, historic forts, craters, museums, brown sandy beaches, and thermal pools. Santa Maria is the oldest while São Miguel is the largest.

Adventure enthusiasts will delight in their options. It has everything but tourists! Go swimming with dolphins, whale watching (June – Sept), fishing, take a jeep safari, enjoy a nature tour, go motor-quading, opt for a donkey ride, explore botanical gardens, go yachting, paragliding, bird watching, diving, canyoning, volcano hiking at Sete Cidades, surfing, biking, and sailing. A must for adventure travelers is to explore the longest lava tube in Europe.

The Azores is also a great place to sunbathe, shop, drink a specialty beer, sample delicious Mediterranean cuisine (such as Cozida, a stew cooked by the heat of the geysers), or attend one of the many festivals held here.

What You Need To Know: All
visitors fly into the Ponta Delgada
International Airport on São Miguel
Island.

How: http://www.azores.com/

Sao Miguel Island

TERRANCE ZEPKE

Notes

Notes

TERRANCE ZEPKE

 Notes

Index

Dolphins Plus
  Research
  Center, 104
Dry Tortugas, 14,
  35, 36, 77, 94,
  145, 176, 177,
  244, 263, 275,
  298
Dry Tortugas
  National Park.
  See Dry
  Tortugas
Duck Key, 125
Duval Street, 11,
  35, 52, 187,
  194, 195, 196,
  207, 212, 237

East Martello
  Museum &
  Gardens, 177
eco-tours, 31, 53,
  80, 237
Ernest
  Hemingway,
  173, 182, 183,
  210, 217, 244
Ernest
  Hemingway

Home and
  Museum, 182
Everglades City,
  56, 74
Everglades
  Museum, 58
Everglades
  National Park,
  53, 55, 60, 68,
  69, 72, 74, 284

Fat Albert, 150
Fat Deer Key, 122
festivals, 12, 216,
  299, 346
fishing, 41, 47,
  49, 58, 80, 84,
  101, 108, 110,
  116, 123, 134,
  135, 147, 152,
  161, 208, 242,
  321, 345
fishing license,
  109
Flagler Station
  Museum, 183
Flamingo, 62
Florida Bay, 19,
  60, 65, 104,

TERRANCE TALKS TRAVEL:
A POCKET GUIDE TO THE
FLORIDA KEYS

Safari Publishing

42958641R00185

Made in the USA
San Bernardino, CA
12 December 2016